ELITE MILITARY UNITS

CHOCTAW CODE TALKERS

Elite Secret Messengers of World War I

by Blake Hoena
illustrated by Maddi Coyne

CAPSTONE PRESS
a capstone imprint

Published by Capstone Press, an imprint of Capstone
1710 Roe Crest Drive, North Mankato, Minnesota 56003
capstonepub.com

Copyright © 2026 by Capstone. All rights reserved. No part of this publication may be reproduced in whole or in part, or stored in a retrieval system, or transmitted in any form or by any means, electronic, mechanical, photocopying, recording, or otherwise, without written permission of the publisher.

Library of Congress Cataloging-in-Publication Data is available
on the Library of Congress website.

ISBN: 9798875215742 (hardcover)
ISBN: 9798875215698 (paperback)
ISBN: 9798875215704 (ebook PDF)

Summary: In this action-packed graphic novel, readers discover the incredible story of the Choctaw Code Talkers during World War I. When the U.S. Army needed a way to communicate military plans securely, they turned to a group of Choctaw soldiers to use their native language to create unbreakable codes. Follow these brave individuals as they fight on the front lines and outsmart the enemy using their little-known language as a secret weapon. Their efforts helped change the course of World War I and paved the way for future Indigenous code talkers.

Editorial Credits:
Editor: Donald Lemke; Designer: Jaime Willems; Production Specialist: Katy LaVigne

Image Credits:
Getty Images: duncan1890 (map background), back cover and throughout, spxChrome (old paper), cover and throughout; Indiana University Museum of Archaeology and Anthropology: Wanamaker Collection/Joseph K. Dixon (#962-08-6451), 4

Any additional websites and resources referenced in this book are not maintained, authorized, or sponsored by Capstone. All product and company names are trademarks™ or registered® trademarks of their respective holders.

Printed and bound in the USA. 6307

TABLE OF CONTENTS

Choctaw Code Talkers 4

Chapter One:
The Choctaw Nation 6

Chapter Two:
The Great War 10

Chapter Three:
The Need for a Code..............................12

Chapter Four:
Call of Duty 16

Chapter Five:
After the War 28

Glossary..30

Read More..31

Internet Sites 31

About the Author 32

About the Illustrator 32

CHOCTAW CODE TALKERS

Unit Name:
36th Infantry Division / 142nd Infantry Regiment

Nickname:
Choctaw Code Talkers

Origin:
Choctaw Nation, primarily from Oklahoma, United States

Years of Service:
1918-1919

Key Missions:
- Meuse-Argonne Offensive (1918)
- Battle of Saint-Étienne (1918)

What They're Known For:
- First Indigenous American unit to use their language as a military code during World War I

- Played a key role in securing American battlefield communications and outmaneuvering German forces

Awards:
- Chevalier de L'Ordre National du Mérite (1989)

- Congressional Gold Medal (2013)

Distinguished Member:
Solomon Bond Lewis, a key member of the Choctaw Code Talkers, helped transmit secret messages during crucial battles. His work, along with that of his fellow Code Talkers, paved the way for future Indigenous code talkers in U.S. military history.

CHAPTER ONE: THE CHOCTAW NATION

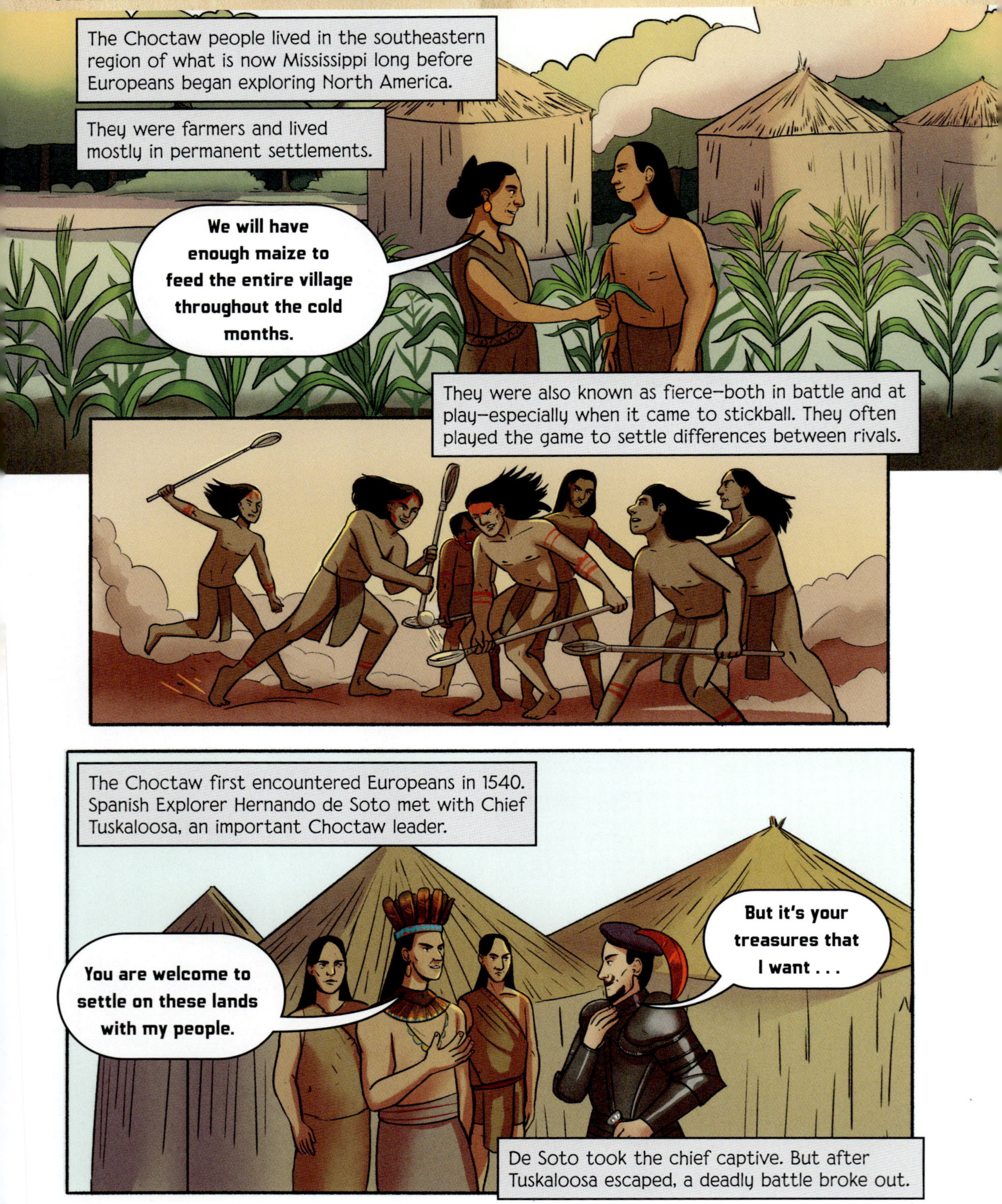
The Choctaw people lived in the southeastern region of what is now Mississippi long before Europeans began exploring North America.
They were farmers and lived mostly in permanent settlements.
We will have enough maize to feed the entire village throughout the cold months.
They were also known as fierce—both in battle and at play—especially when it came to stickball. They often played the game to settle differences between rivals.
The Choctaw first encountered Europeans in 1540. Spanish Explorer Hernando de Soto met with Chief Tuskaloosa, an important Choctaw leader.
You are welcome to settle on these lands with my people.
But it's your treasures that I want . . .
De Soto took the chief captive. But after Tuskaloosa escaped, a deadly battle broke out.

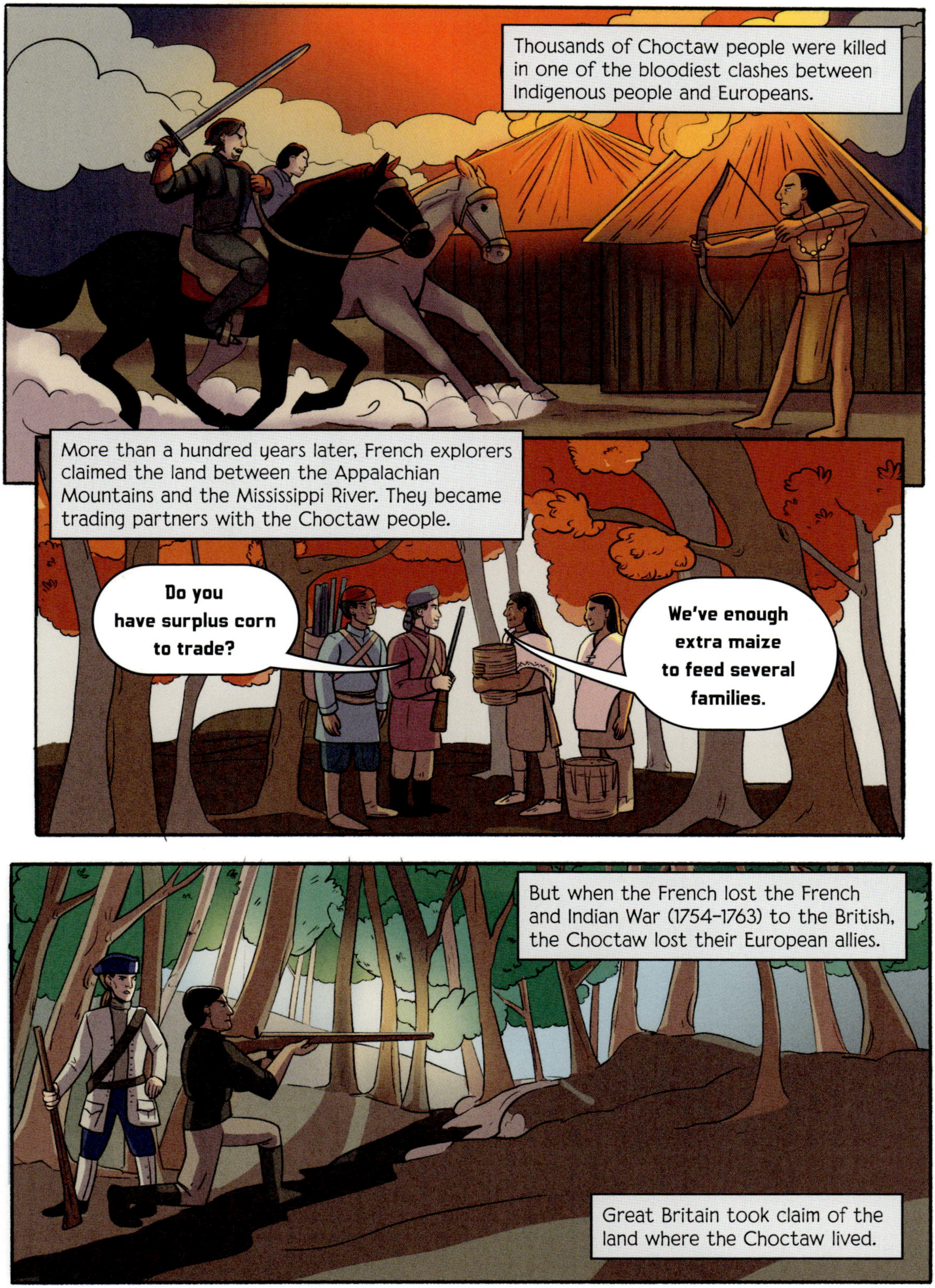
Thousands of Choctaw people were killed in one of the bloodiest clashes between Indigenous people and Europeans.
More than a hundred years later, French explorers claimed the land between the Appalachian Mountains and the Mississippi River. They became trading partners with the Choctaw people.
Do you have surplus corn to trade?
We've enough extra maize to feed several families.
But when the French lost the French and Indian War (1754–1763) to the British, the Choctaw lost their European allies.
Great Britain took claim of the land where the Choctaw lived.

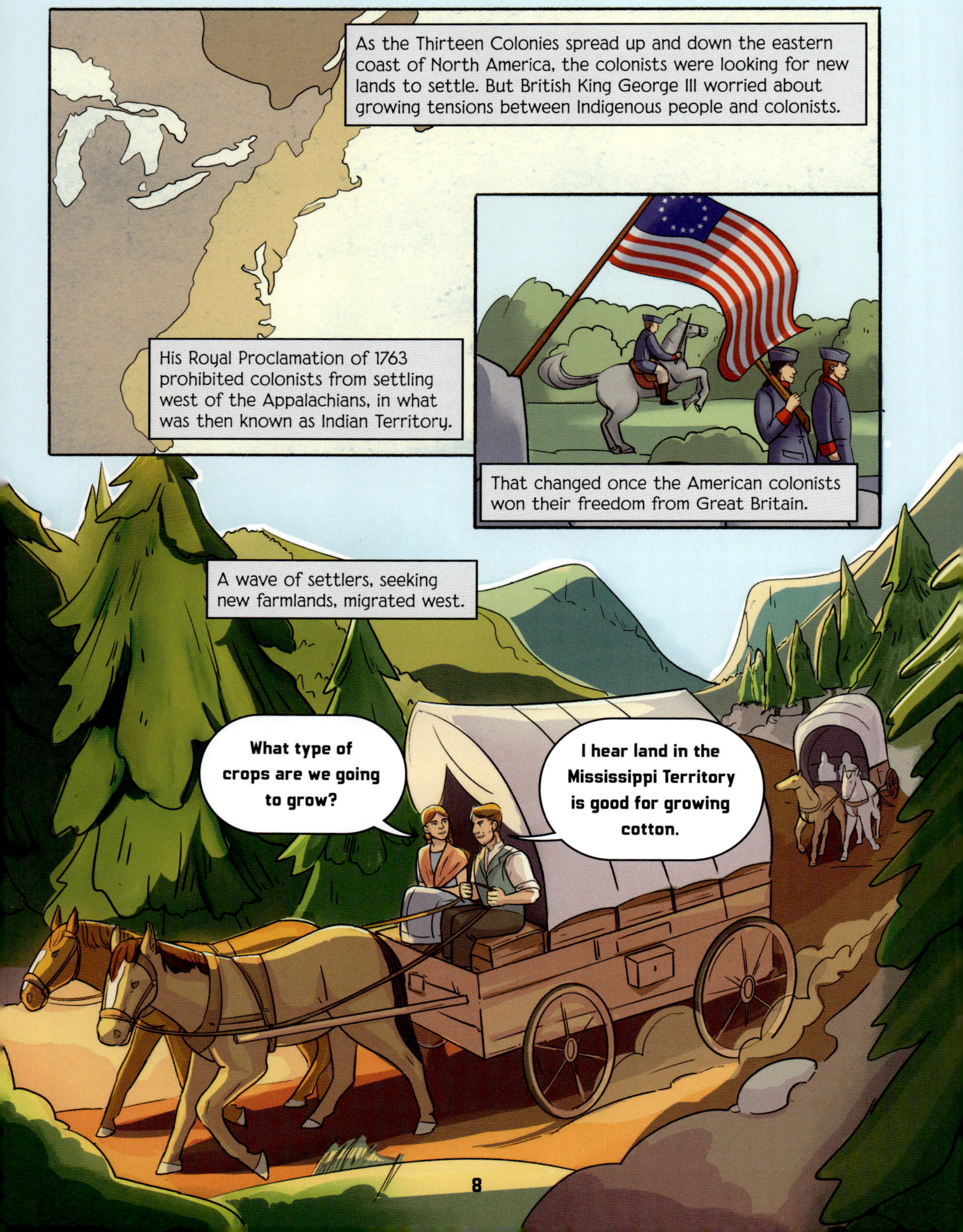

As the Thirteen Colonies spread up and down the eastern coast of North America, the colonists were looking for new lands to settle. But British King George III worried about growing tensions between Indigenous people and colonists.
His Royal Proclamation of 1763 prohibited colonists from settling west of the Appalachians, in what was then known as Indian Territory.
That changed once the American colonists won their freedom from Great Britain.
A wave of settlers, seeking new farmlands, migrated west.
What type of crops are we going to grow?
I hear land in the Mississippi Territory is good for growing cotton.

The U.S. government took Choctaw land through treaties, such as the Treaty of Fort Adams. For only a few thousand dollars' worth of goods, the Choctaw lost millions of acres of land.
Here are the tools we are giving you as part of this treaty.
Treaty after treaty, more land was taken from the Choctaw.
Then in 1830, the U.S. Congress passed the Indian Removal Act. The Choctaw were the first Indigenous people to be forced from their traditional land.
Granddaughter, you must leave me behind. I can't go on.
But, Grandfather . . . I can't lose you.
They were set on a path west that would become known as the Trail of Tears. Thousands died from disease and starvation along the way.
At the end of the long, harsh journey, the Choctaw were relocated to a reservation in Oklahoma.
Today, most Choctaw live on an 11,000-square-mile (28,500-square-kilometer) reservation in southeastern Oklahoma, but some remain in Mississippi.

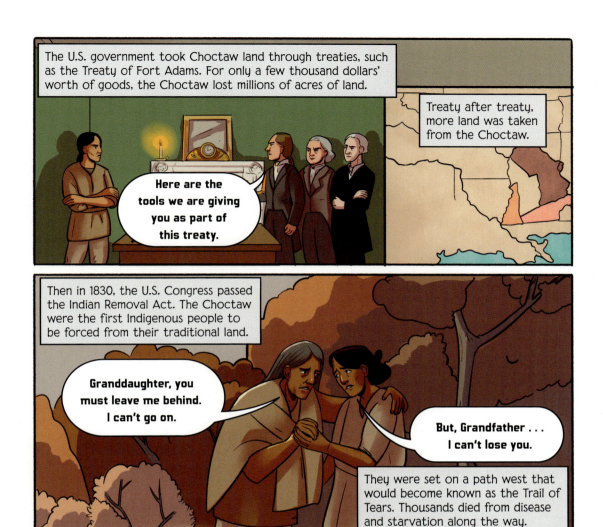

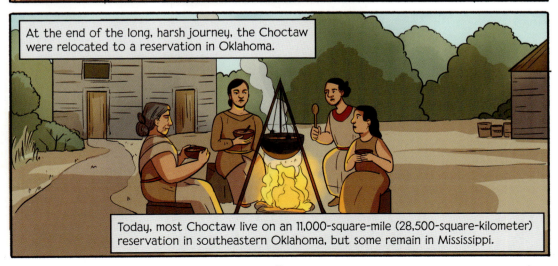

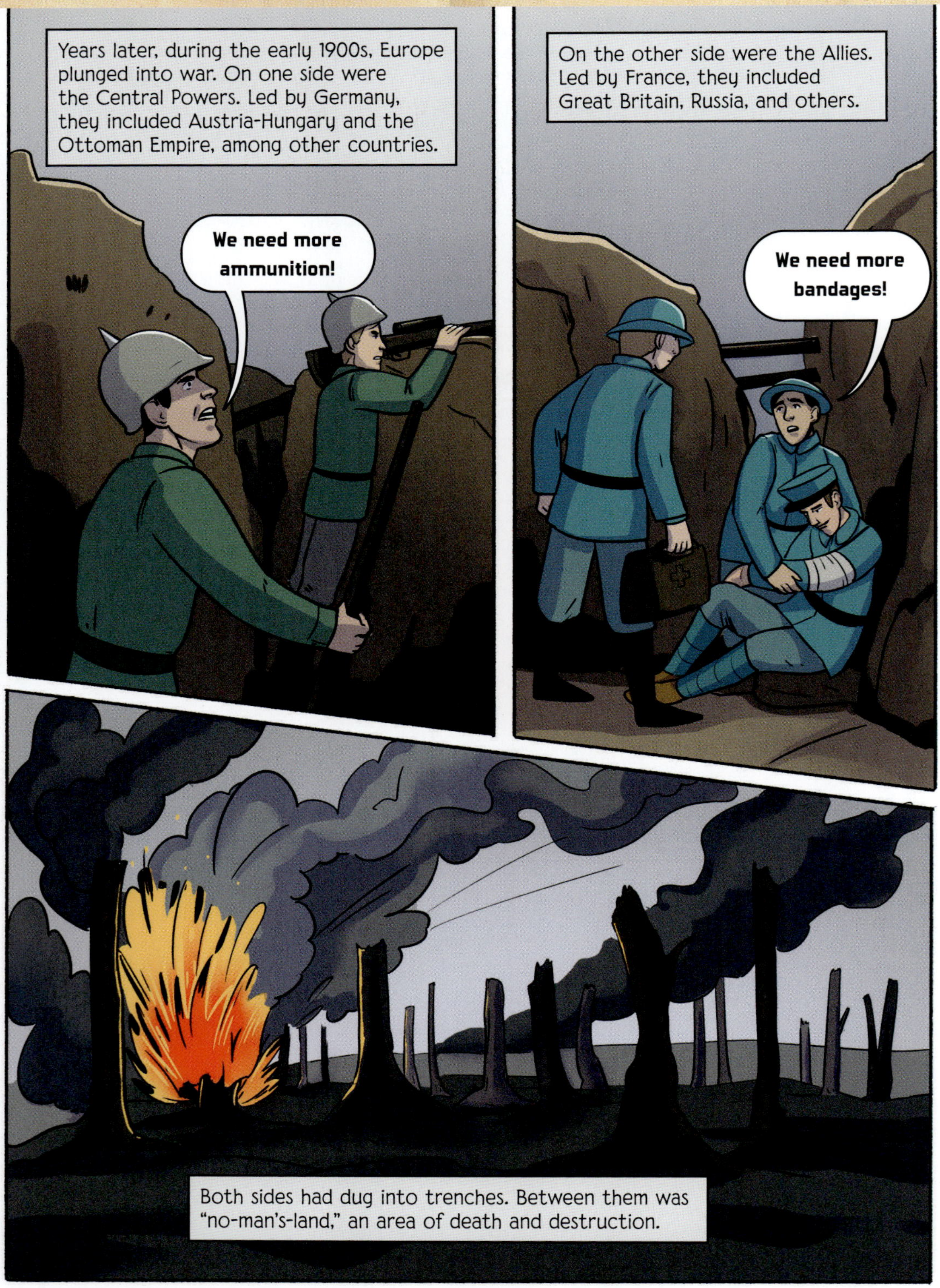
Years later, during the early 1900s, Europe plunged into war. On one side were the Central Powers. Led by Germany, they included Austria-Hungary and the Ottoman Empire, among other countries.
We need more ammunition!
On the other side were the Allies. Led by France, they included Great Britain, Russia, and others.
We need more bandages!
Both sides had dug into trenches. Between them was "no-man's-land," an area of death and destruction.

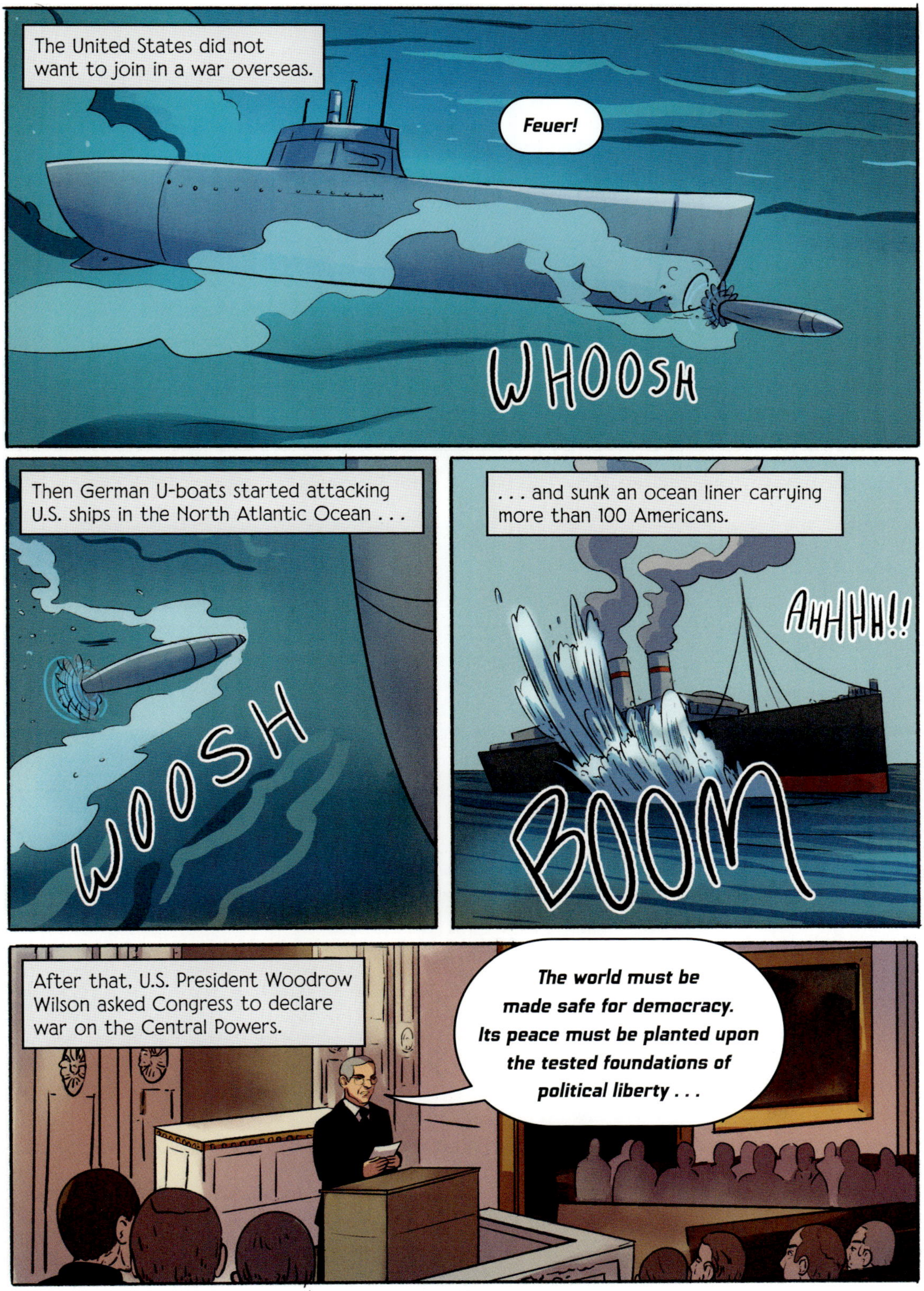
The United States did not want to join in a war overseas.
Feuer!
WHOOSH
Then German U-boats started attacking U.S. ships in the North Atlantic Ocean . . .
WOOSH
. . . and sunk an ocean liner carrying more than 100 Americans.
AHHHH!!
BOOM
After that, U.S. President Woodrow Wilson asked Congress to declare war on the Central Powers.
The world must be made safe for democracy. Its peace must be planted upon the tested foundations of political liberty . . .

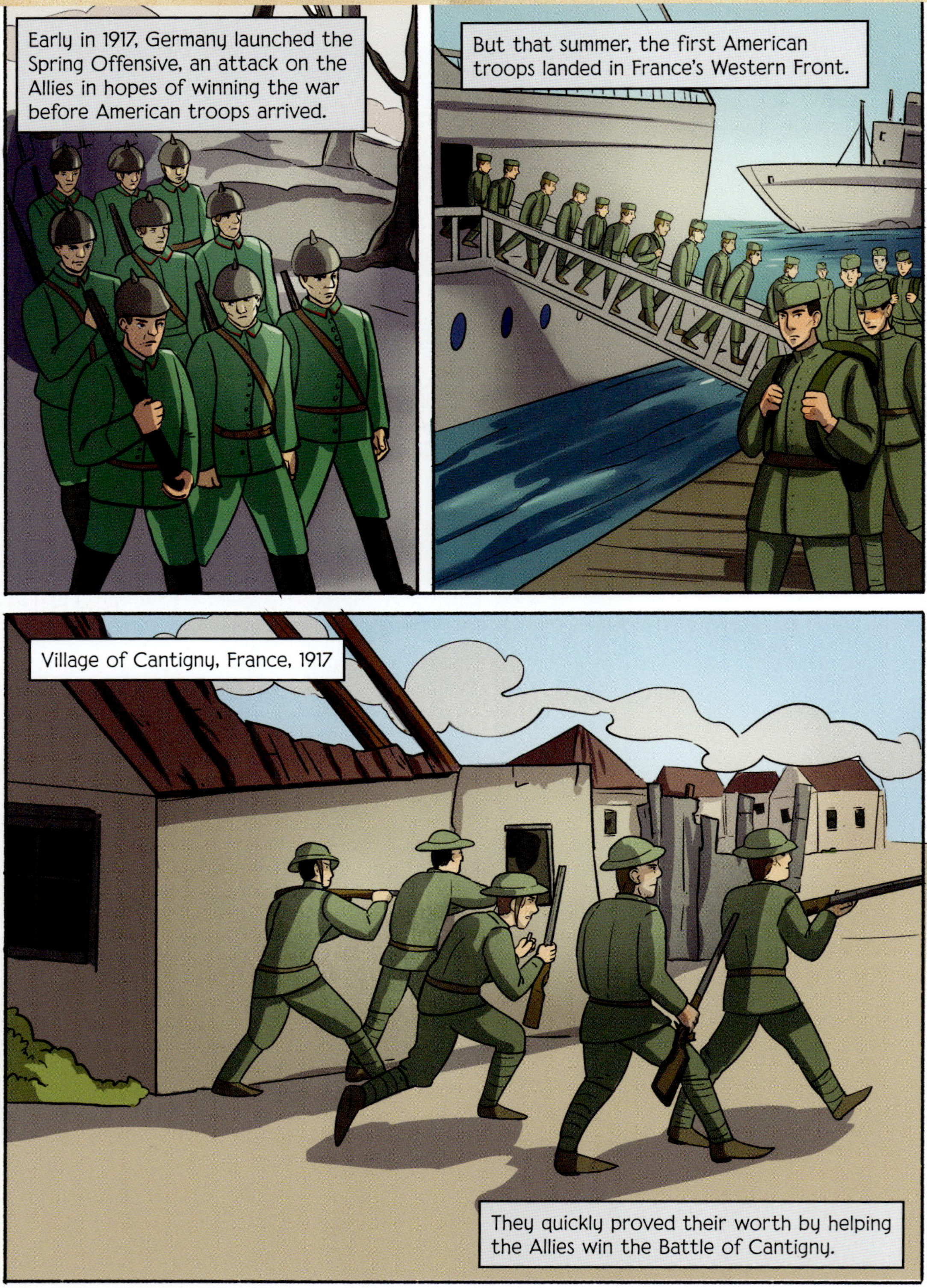
Early in 1917, Germany launched the Spring Offensive, an attack on the Allies in hopes of winning the war before American troops arrived.
But that summer, the first American troops landed in France's Western Front.
Village of Cantigny, France, 1917
They quickly proved their worth by helping the Allies win the Battle of Cantigny.

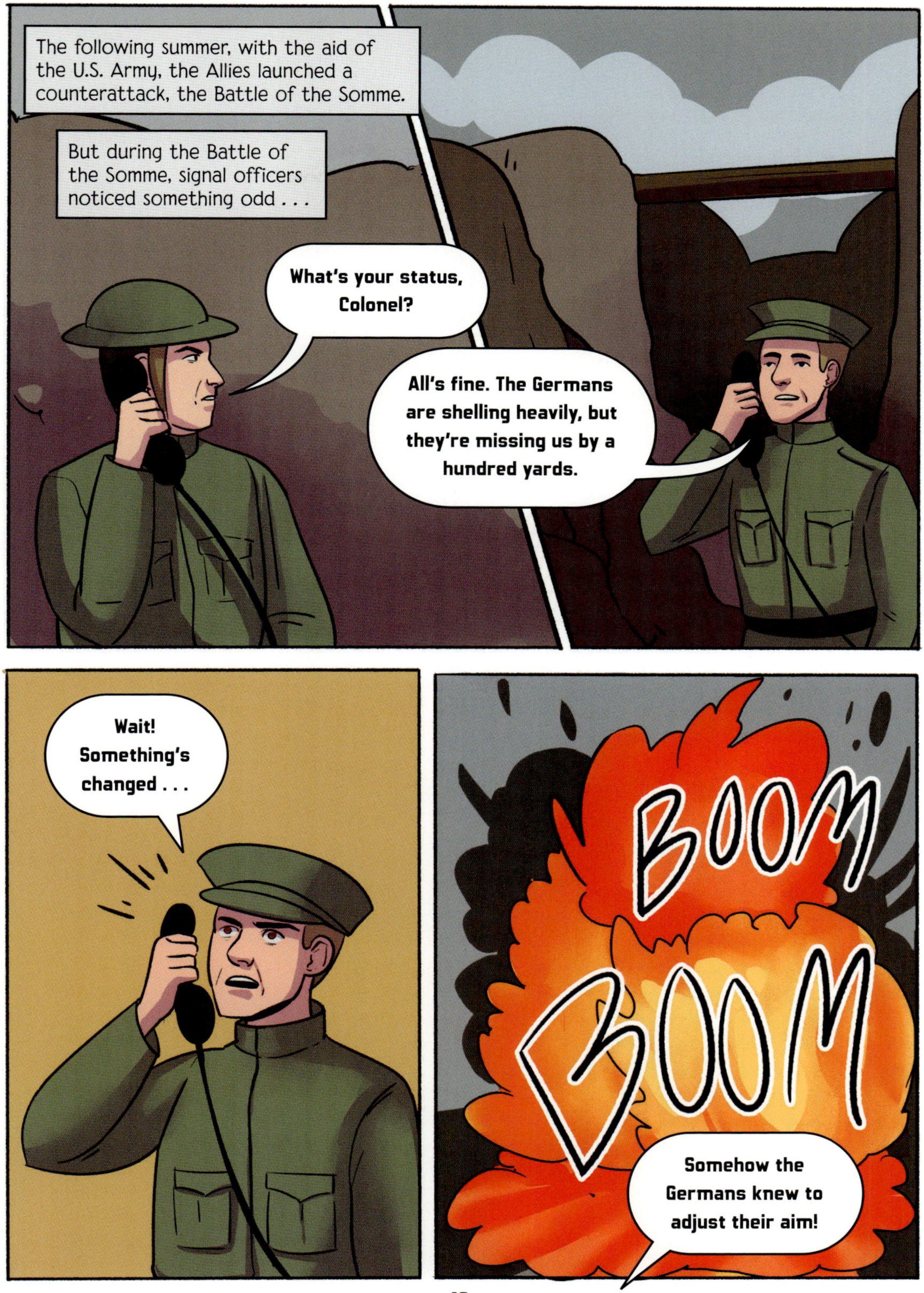
The following summer, with the aid of the U.S. Army, the Allies launched a counterattack, the Battle of the Somme.
But during the Battle of the Somme, signal officers noticed something odd . . .
What's your status, Colonel?
All's fine. The Germans are shelling heavily, but they're missing us by a hundred yards.
Wait! Something's changed . . .
BOOM
BOOM
Somehow the Germans knew to adjust their aim!

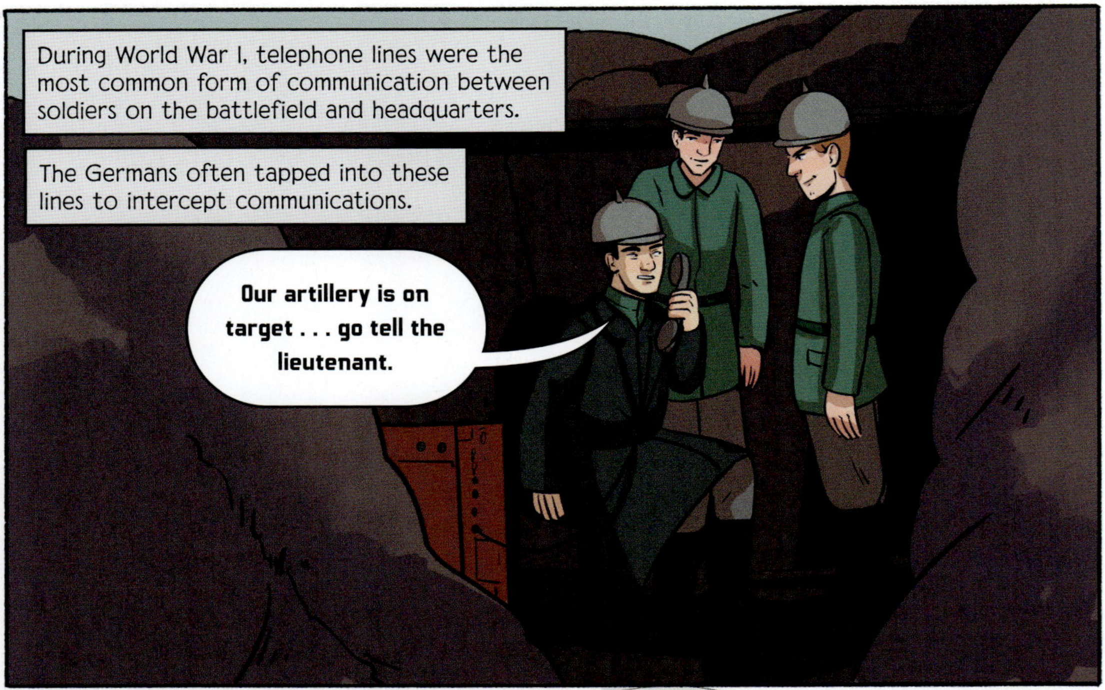
During World War I, telephone lines were the most common form of communication between soldiers on the battlefield and headquarters.
The Germans often tapped into these lines to intercept communications.
Our artillery is on target . . . go tell the lieutenant.

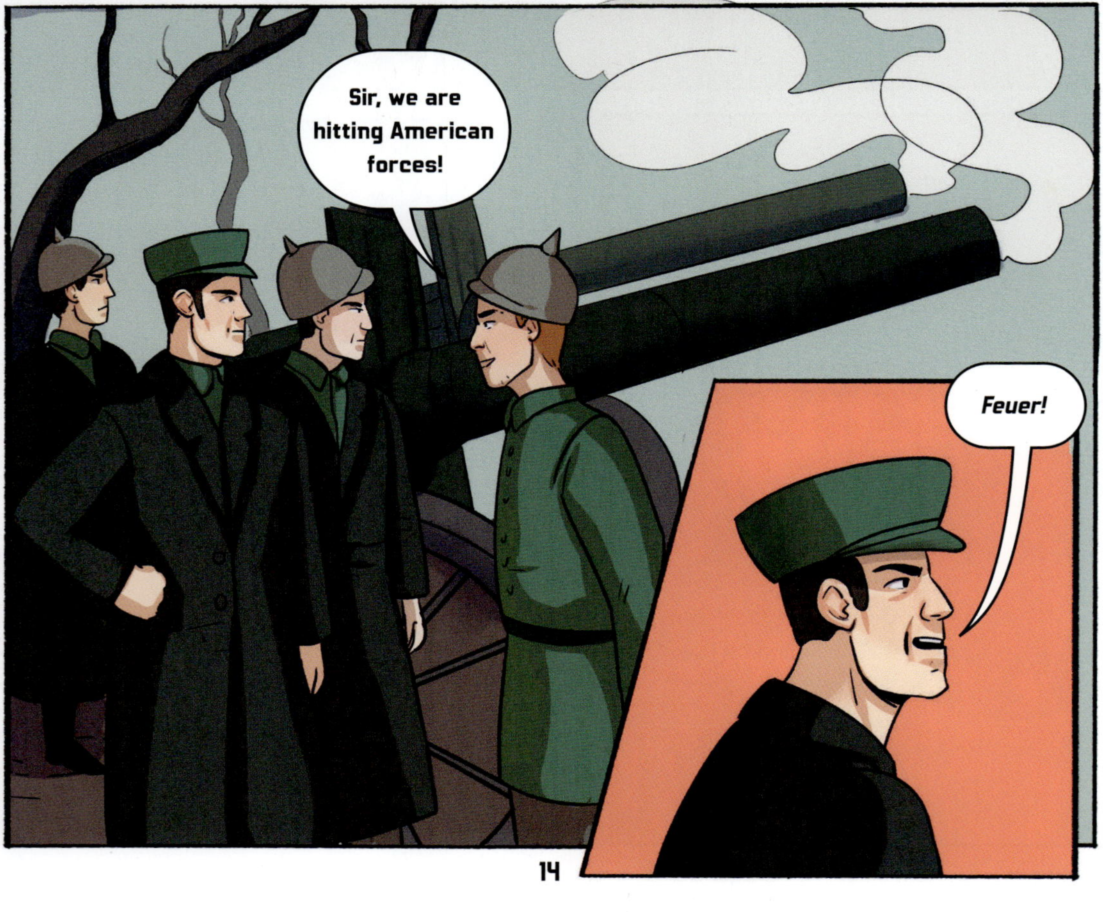
Sir, we are hitting American forces!
Feuer!

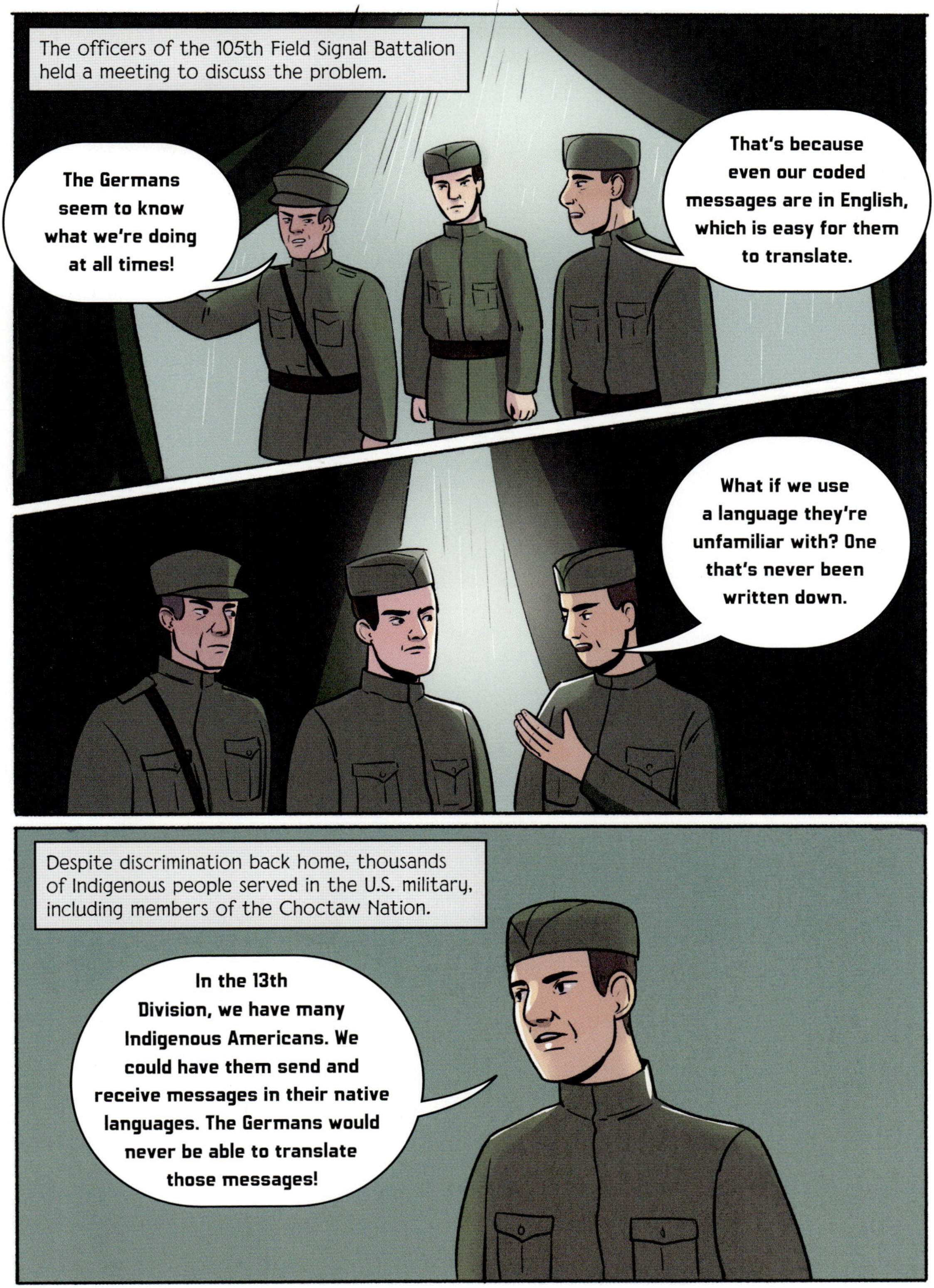

The officers of the 105th Field Signal Battalion held a meeting to discuss the problem.
The Germans seem to know what we're doing at all times!
That's because even our coded messages are in English, which is easy for them to translate.
What if we use a language they're unfamiliar with? One that's never been written down.
Despite discrimination back home, thousands of Indigenous people served in the U.S. military, including members of the Choctaw Nation.
In the 13th Division, we have many Indigenous Americans. We could have them send and receive messages in their native languages. The Germans would never be able to translate those messages!

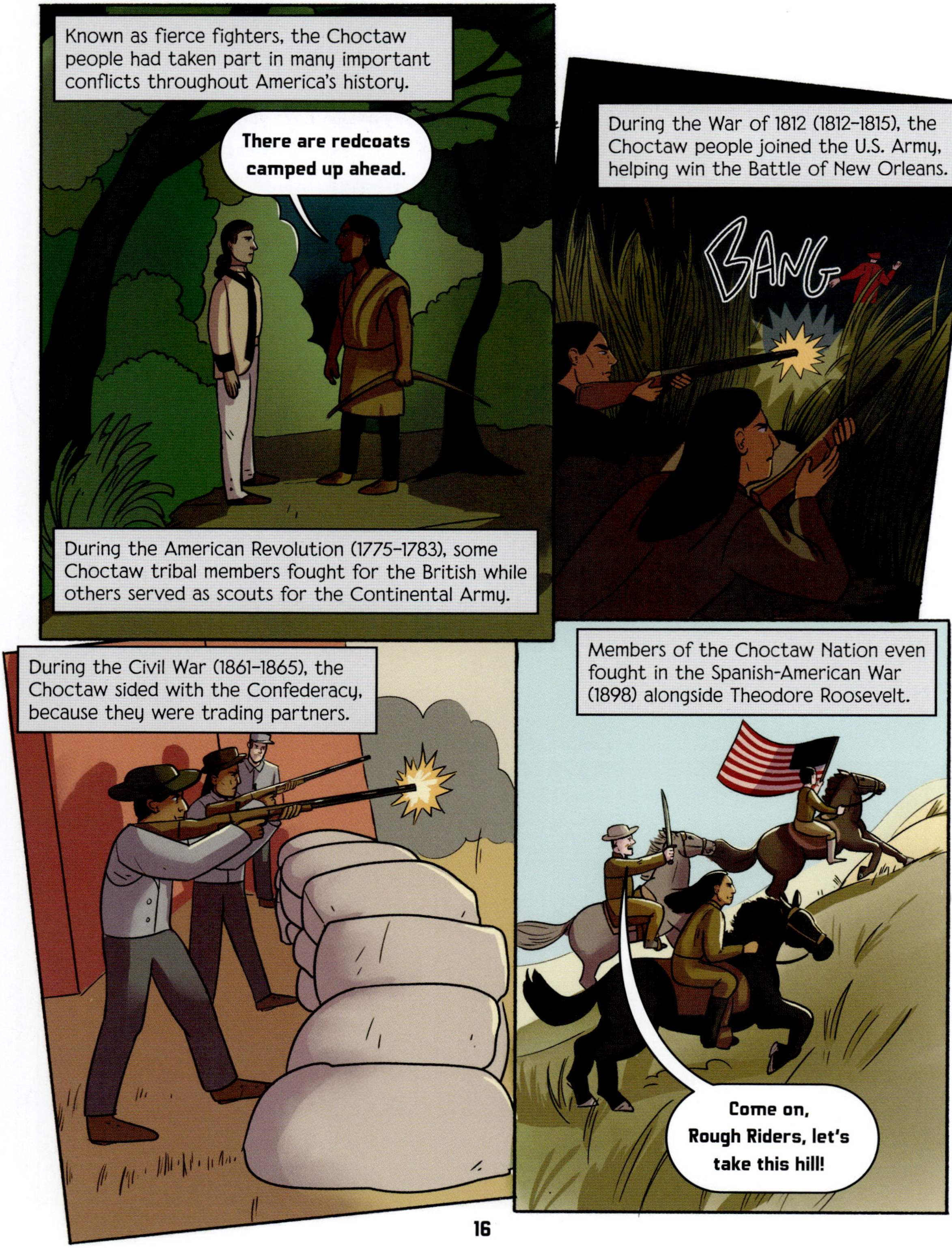
Known as fierce fighters, the Choctaw people had taken part in many important conflicts throughout America's history.
There are redcoats camped up ahead.
During the American Revolution (1775–1783), some Choctaw tribal members fought for the British while others served as scouts for the Continental Army.
During the War of 1812 (1812–1815), the Choctaw people joined the U.S. Army, helping win the Battle of New Orleans.
BANG
During the Civil War (1861–1865), the Choctaw sided with the Confederacy, because they were trading partners.
Members of the Choctaw Nation even fought in the Spanish-American War (1898) alongside Theodore Roosevelt.
Come on, Rough Riders, let's take this hill!

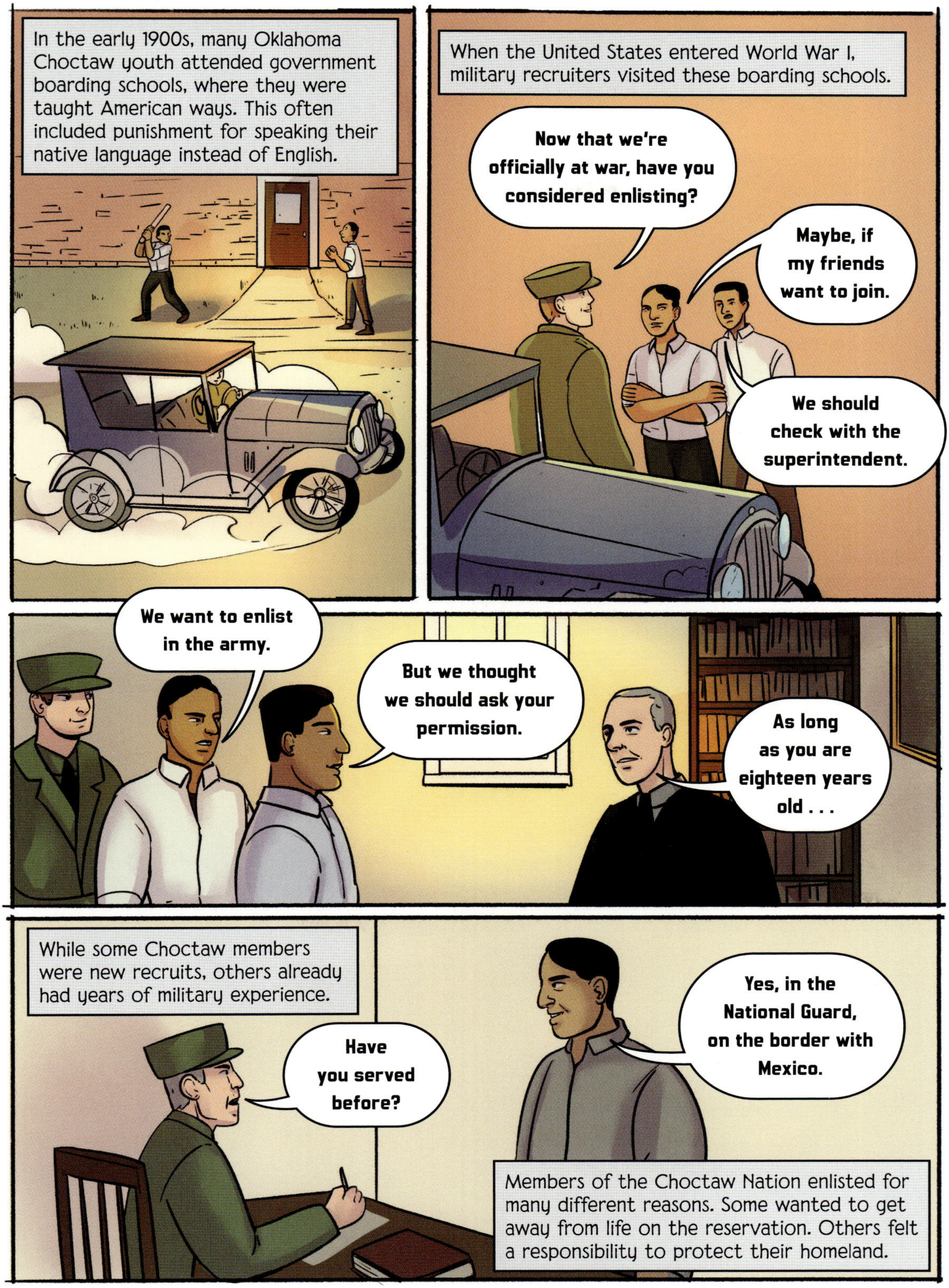
In the early 1900s, many Oklahoma Choctaw youth attended government boarding schools, where they were taught American ways. This often included punishment for speaking their native language instead of English.
When the United States entered World War I, military recruiters visited these boarding schools.
Now that we're officially at war, have you considered enlisting?
Maybe, if my friends want to join.
We should check with the superintendent.
We want to enlist in the army.
But we thought we should ask your permission.
As long as you are eighteen years old . . .
While some Choctaw members were new recruits, others already had years of military experience.
Have you served before?
Yes, in the National Guard, on the border with Mexico.
Members of the Choctaw Nation enlisted for many different reasons. Some wanted to get away from life on the reservation. Others felt a responsibility to protect their homeland.

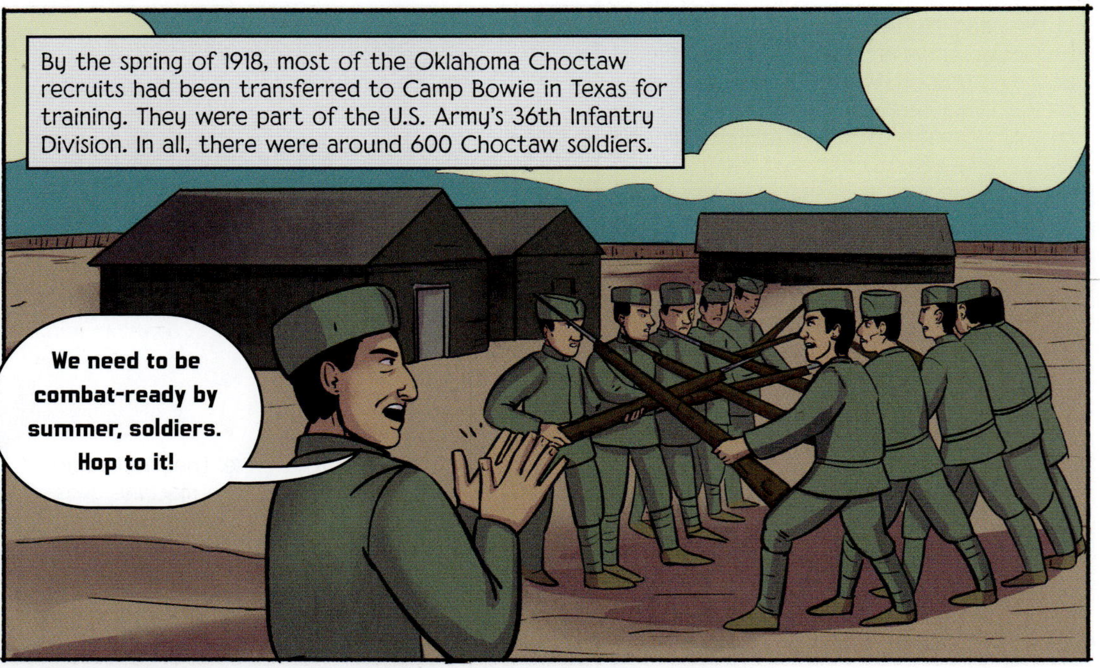
By the spring of 1918, most of the Oklahoma Choctaw recruits had been transferred to Camp Bowie in Texas for training. They were part of the U.S. Army's 36th Infantry Division. In all, there were around 600 Choctaw soldiers.
We need to be combat-ready by summer, soldiers. Hop to it!

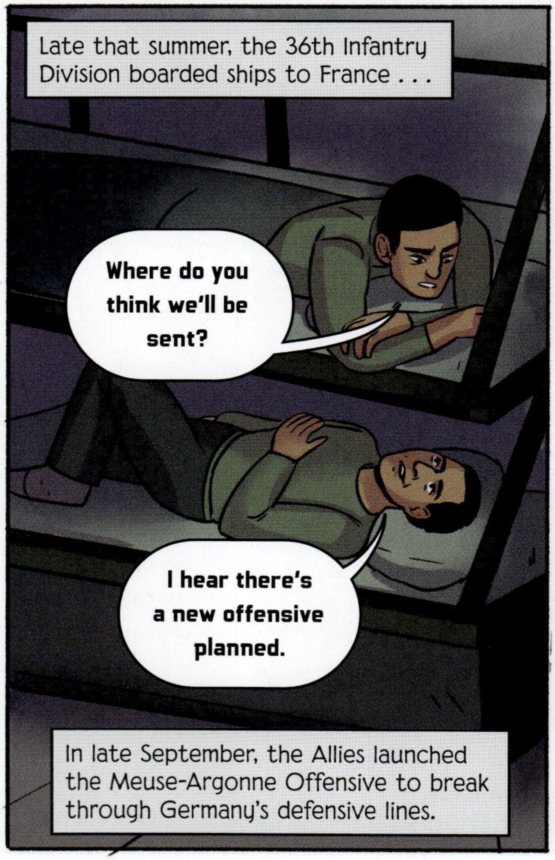
Late that summer, the 36th Infantry Division boarded ships to France . . .
Where do you think we'll be sent?
I hear there's a new offensive planned.
In late September, the Allies launched the Meuse-Argonne Offensive to break through Germany's defensive lines.

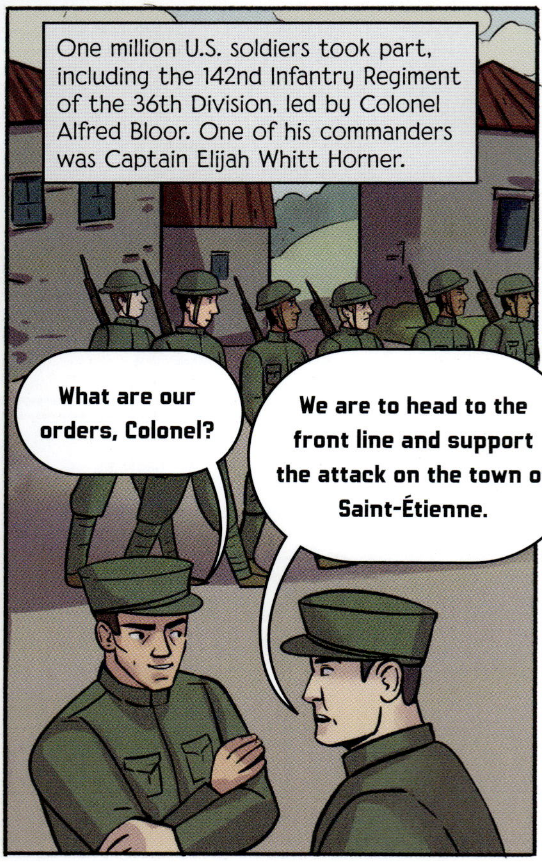
One million U.S. soldiers took part, including the 142nd Infantry Regiment of the 36th Division, led by Colonel Alfred Bloor. One of his commanders was Captain Elijah Whitt Horner.
What are our orders, Colonel?
We are to head to the front line and support the attack on the town of Saint-Étienne.

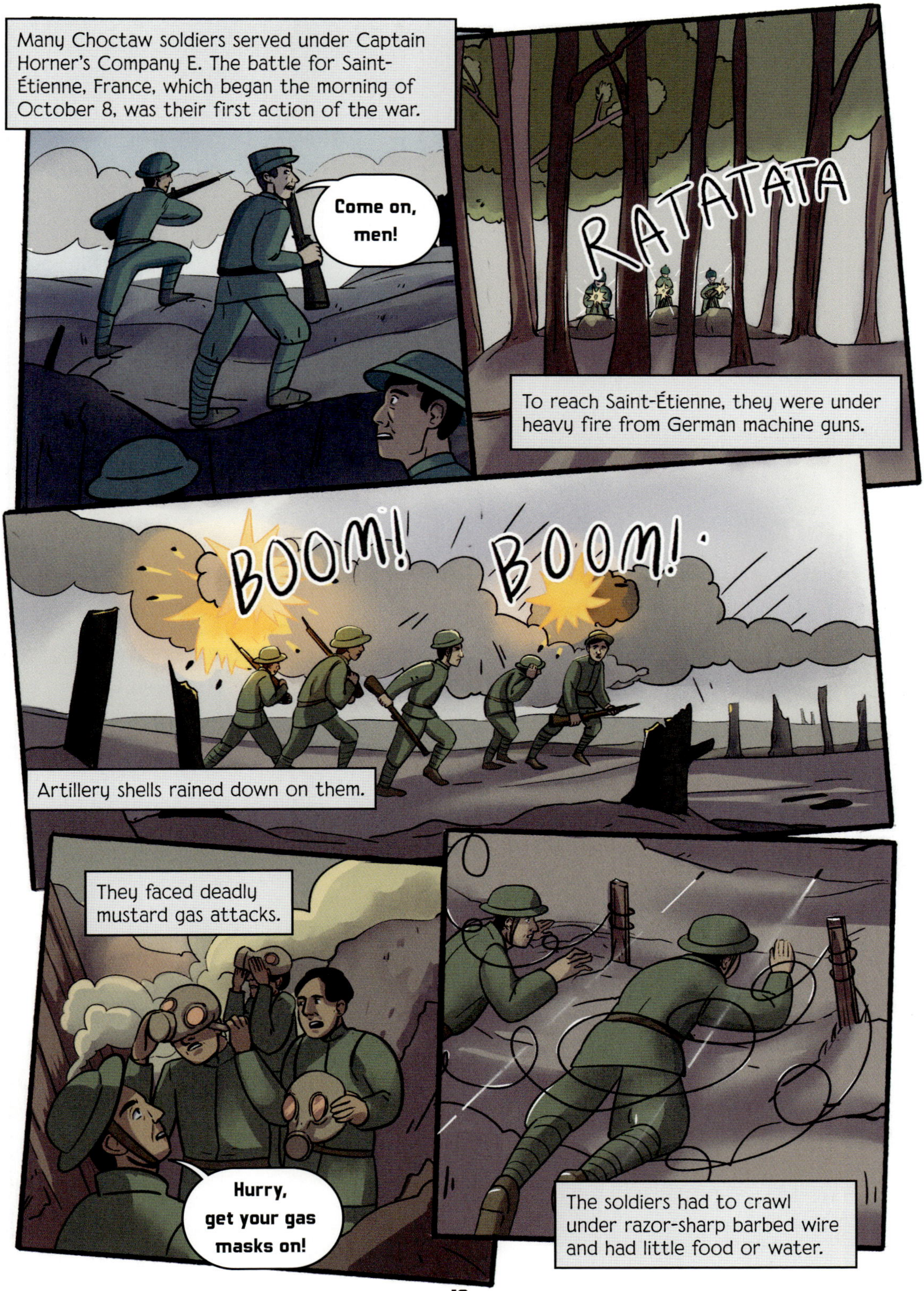
Many Choctaw soldiers served under Captain Horner's Company E. The battle for Saint-Étienne, France, which began the morning of October 8, was their first action of the war.
Come on, men!
RATATATA
To reach Saint-Étienne, they were under heavy fire from German machine guns.
BOOM!
BOOM!
Artillery shells rained down on them.
They faced deadly mustard gas attacks.
Hurry, get your gas masks on!
The soldiers had to crawl under razor-sharp barbed wire and had little food or water.

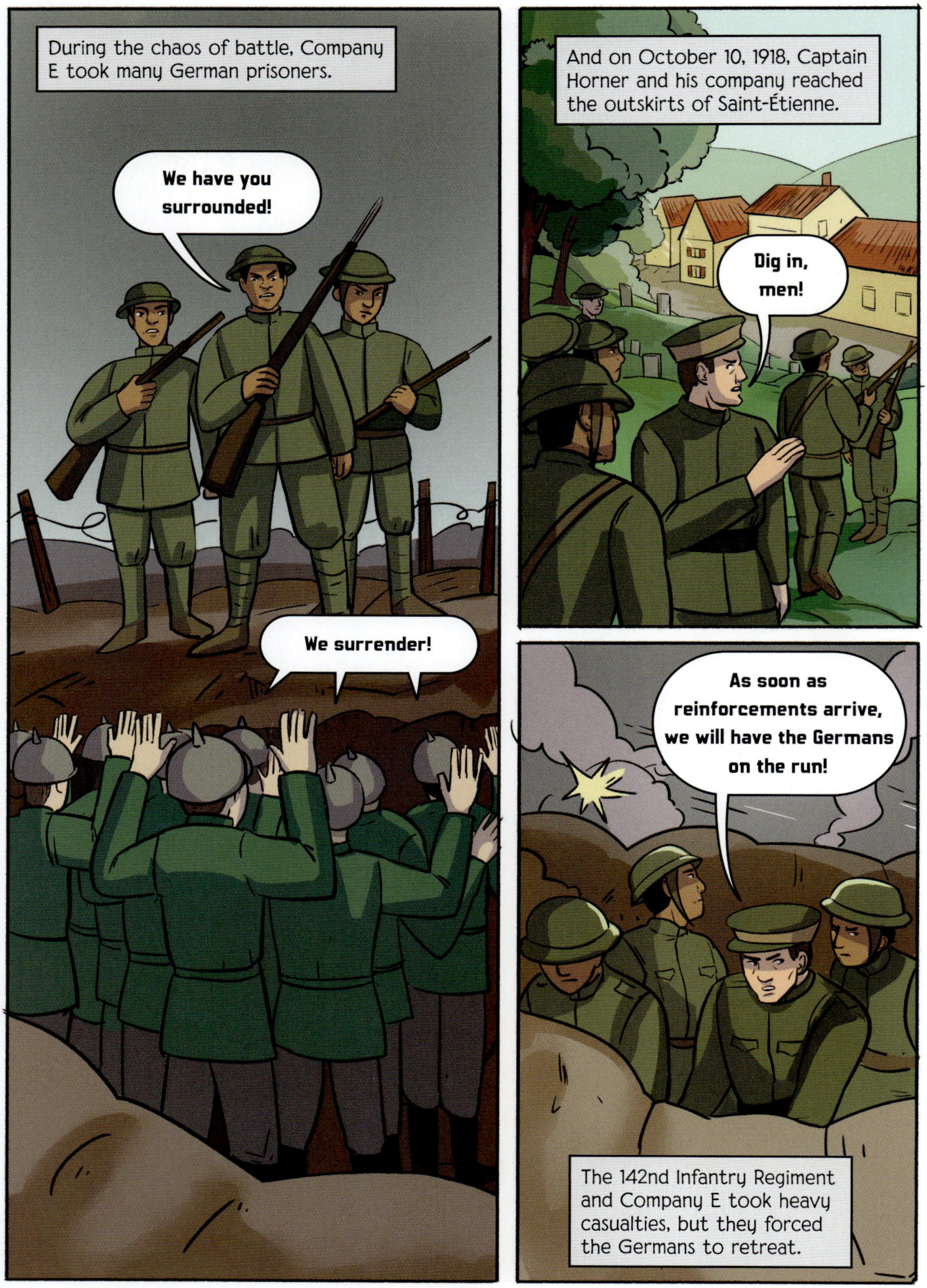
During the chaos of battle, Company E took many German prisoners.
We have you surrounded!
We surrender!
And on October 10, 1918, Captain Horner and his company reached the outskirts of Saint-Étienne.
Dig in, men!
As soon as reinforcements arrive, we will have the Germans on the run!
The 142nd Infantry Regiment and Company E took heavy casualties, but they forced the Germans to retreat.

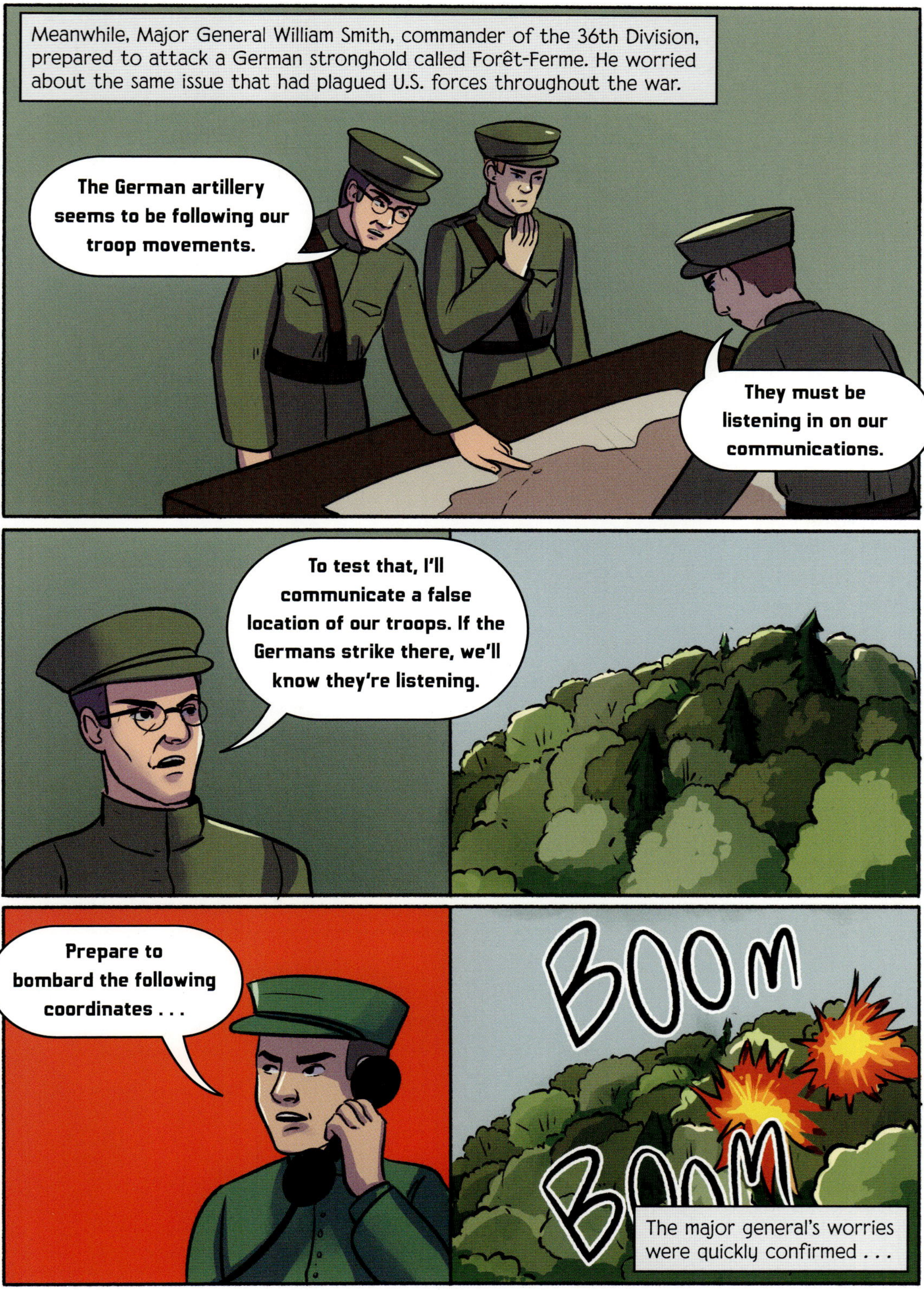
Meanwhile, Major General William Smith, commander of the 36th Division, prepared to attack a German stronghold called Forêt-Ferme. He worried about the same issue that had plagued U.S. forces throughout the war.
The German artillery seems to be following our troop movements.
They must be listening in on our communications.
To test that, I'll communicate a false location of our troops. If the Germans strike there, we'll know they're listening.
Prepare to bombard the following coordinates . . .
BOOM
BOOM
The major general's worries were quickly confirmed . . .

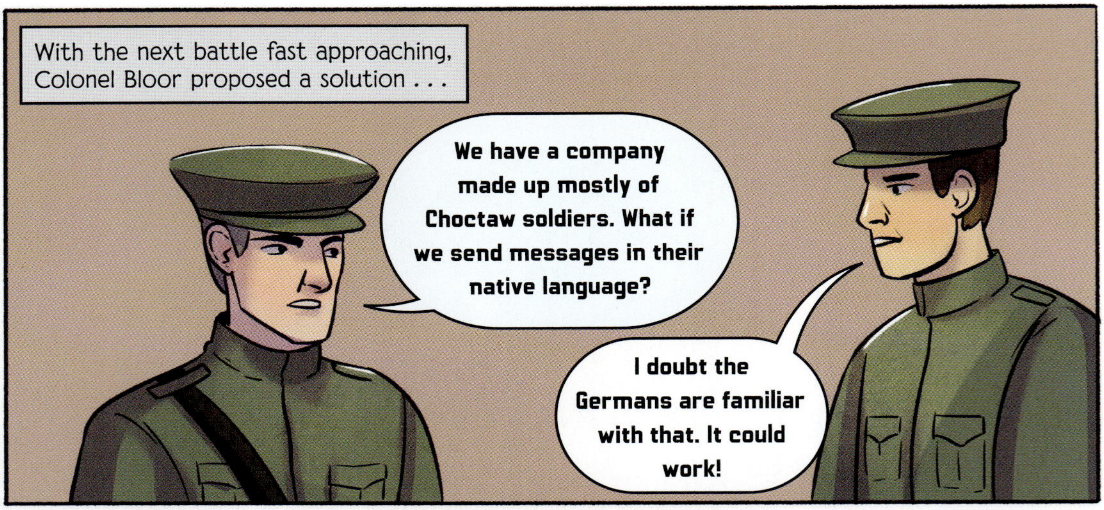
With the next battle fast approaching, Colonel Bloor proposed a solution . . .
We have a company made up mostly of Choctaw soldiers. What if we send messages in their native language?
I doubt the Germans are familiar with that. It could work!

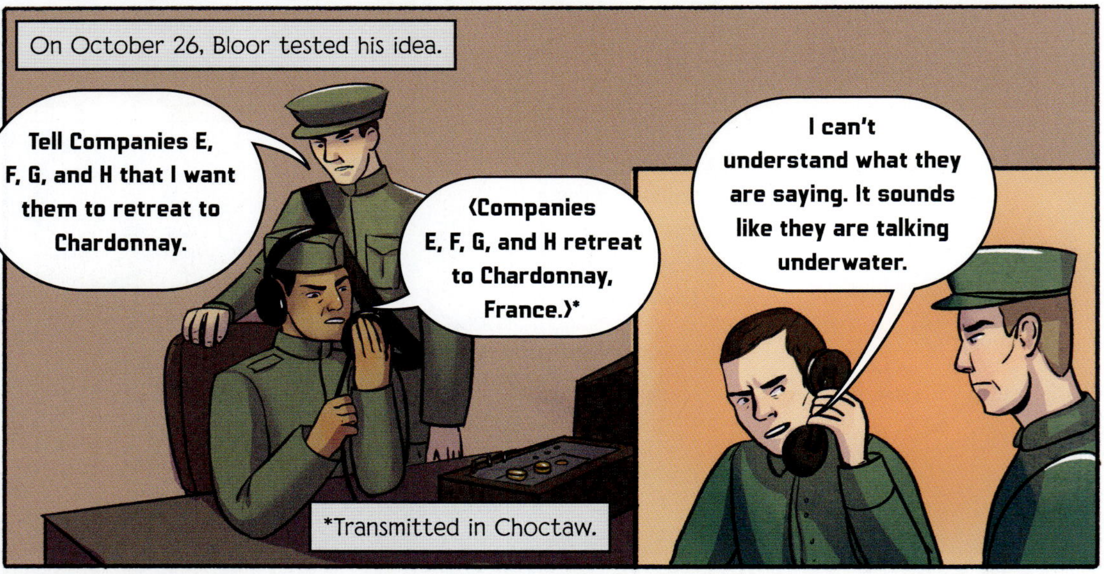
On October 26, Bloor tested his idea.
Tell Companies E, F, G, and H that I want them to retreat to Chardonnay.
⟨Companies E, F, G, and H retreat to Chardonnay, France.⟩*
*Transmitted in Choctaw.
I can't understand what they are saying. It sounds like they are talking underwater.

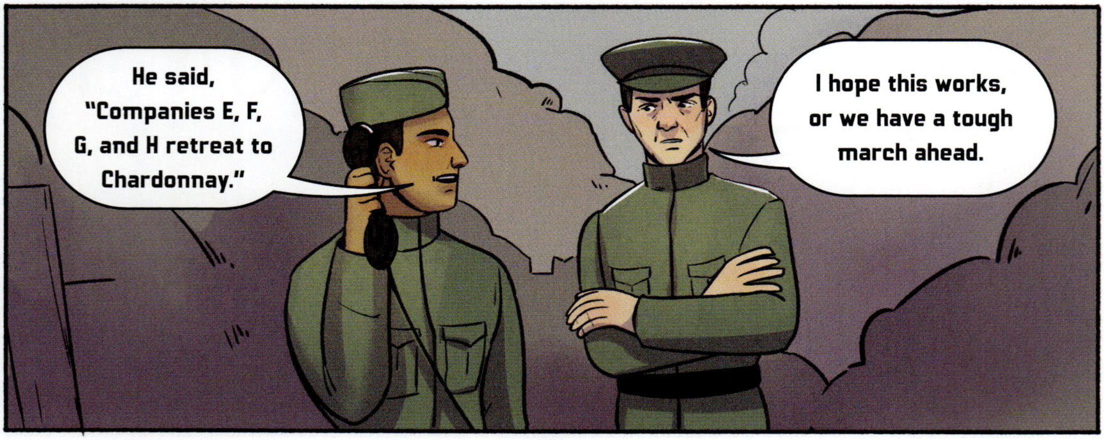
He said, "Companies E, F, G, and H retreat to Chardonnay."
I hope this works, or we have a tough march ahead.

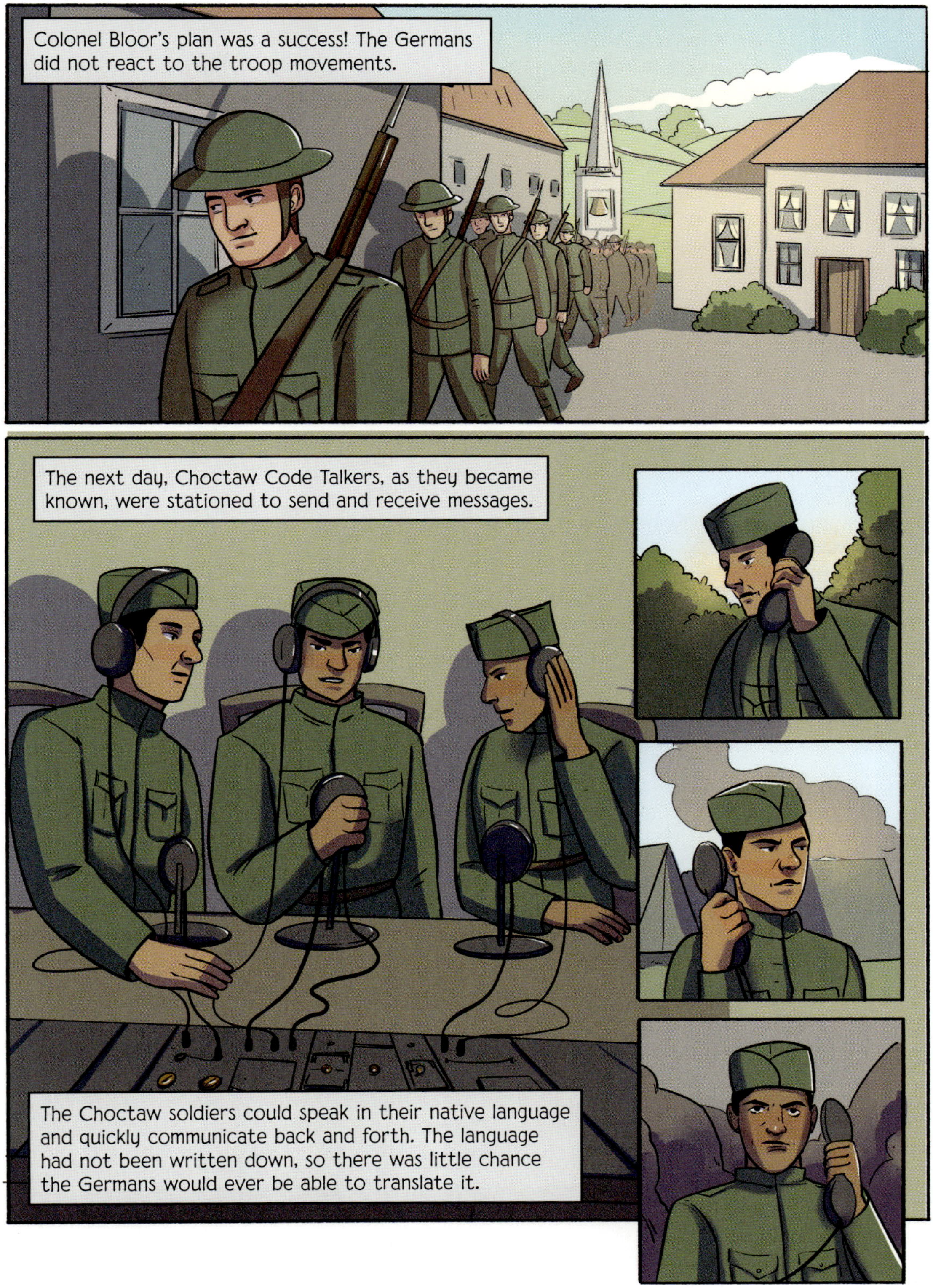
Colonel Bloor's plan was a success! The Germans did not react to the troop movements.
The next day, Choctaw Code Talkers, as they became known, were stationed to send and receive messages.
The Choctaw soldiers could speak in their native language and quickly communicate back and forth. The language had not been written down, so there was little chance the Germans would ever be able to translate it.

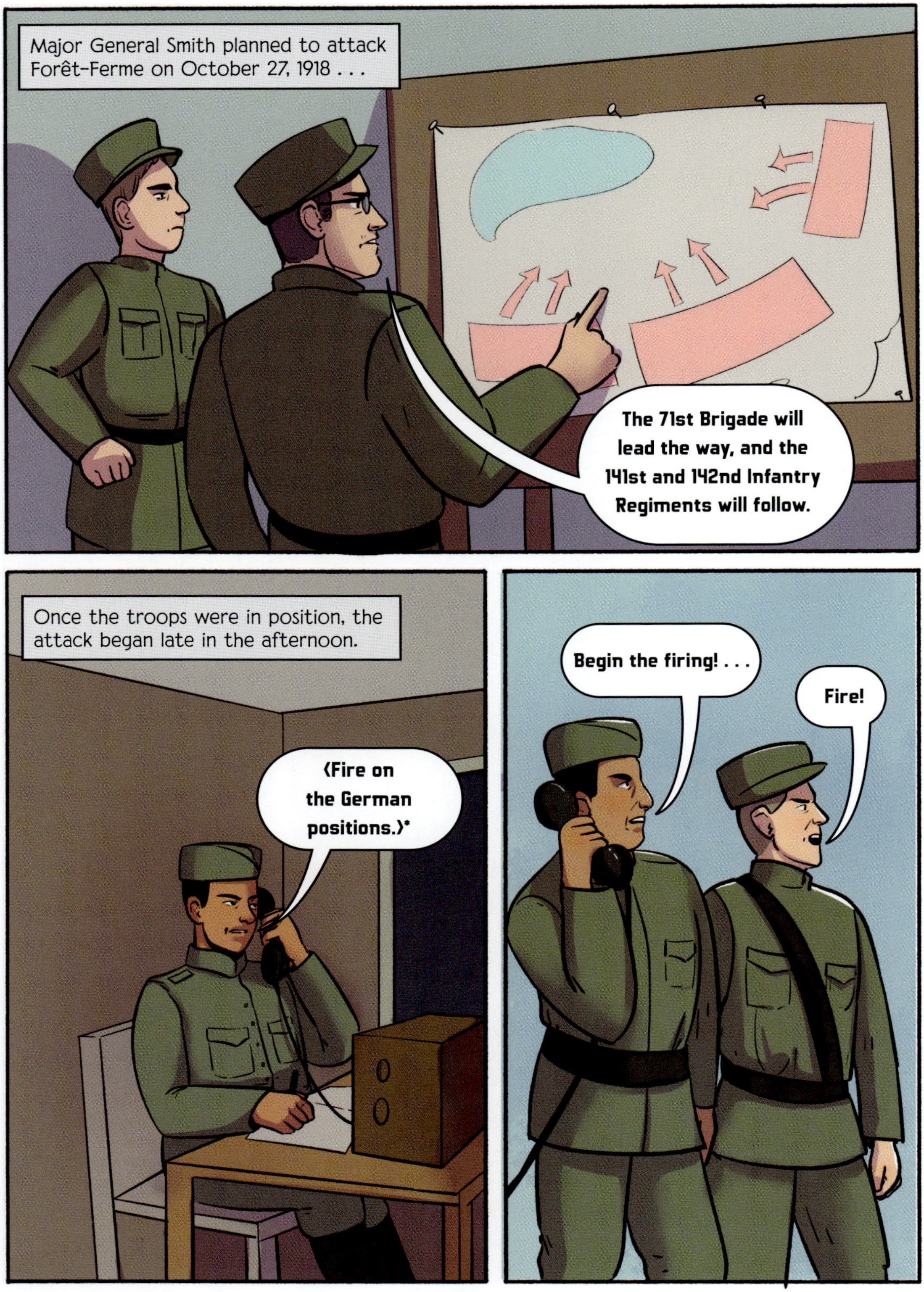
Major General Smith planned to attack Forêt-Ferme on October 27, 1918 . . .
The 71st Brigade will lead the way, and the 141st and 142nd Infantry Regiments will follow.
Once the troops were in position, the attack began late in the afternoon.
‹Fire on the German positions.›*
Begin the firing! . . .
Fire!

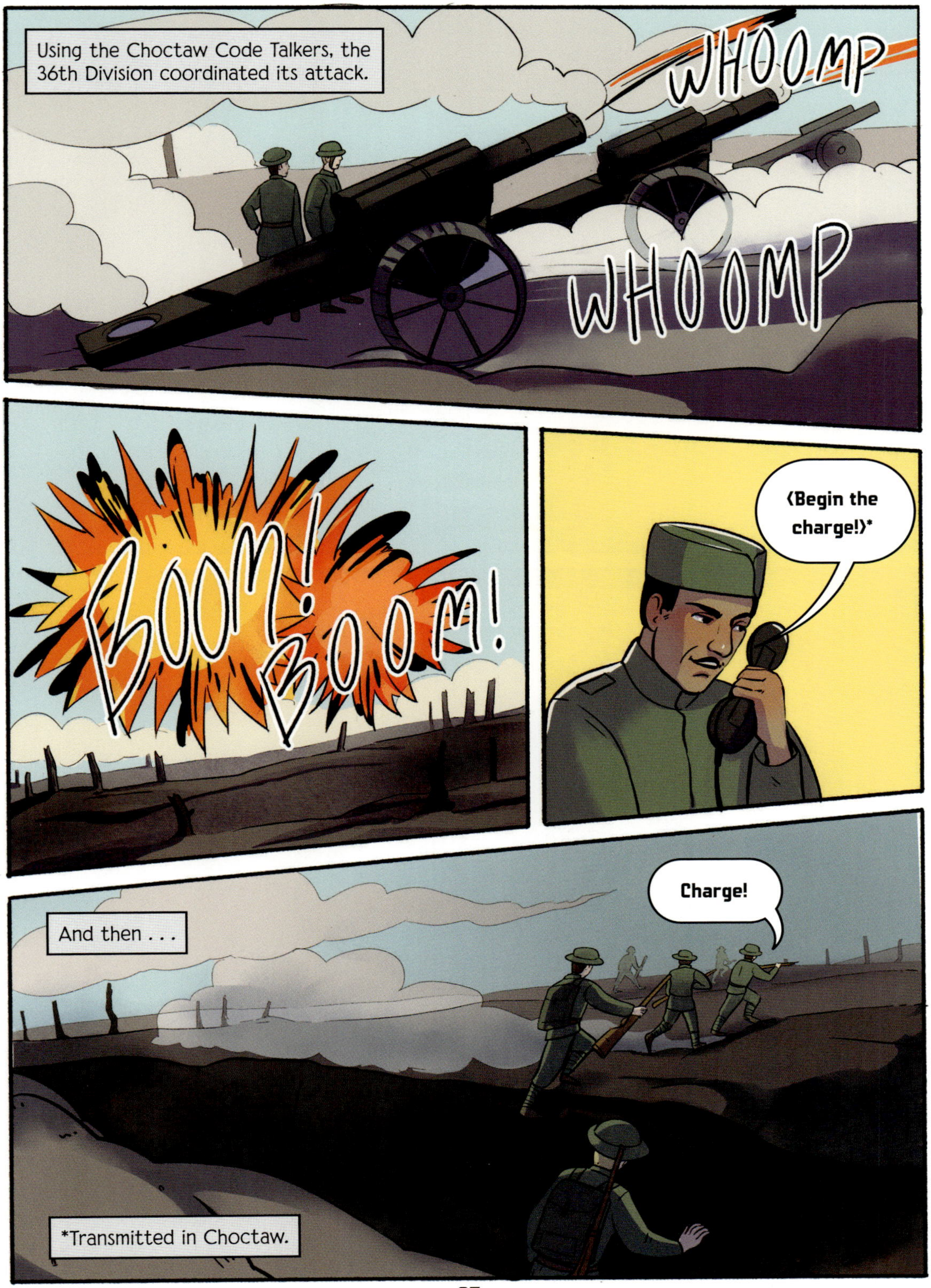

Using the Choctaw Code Talkers, the 36th Division coordinated its attack.
WHOOMP
WHOOMP
BOOM! BOOM!
⟨Begin the charge!⟩*
And then . . .
Charge!
*Transmitted in Choctaw.

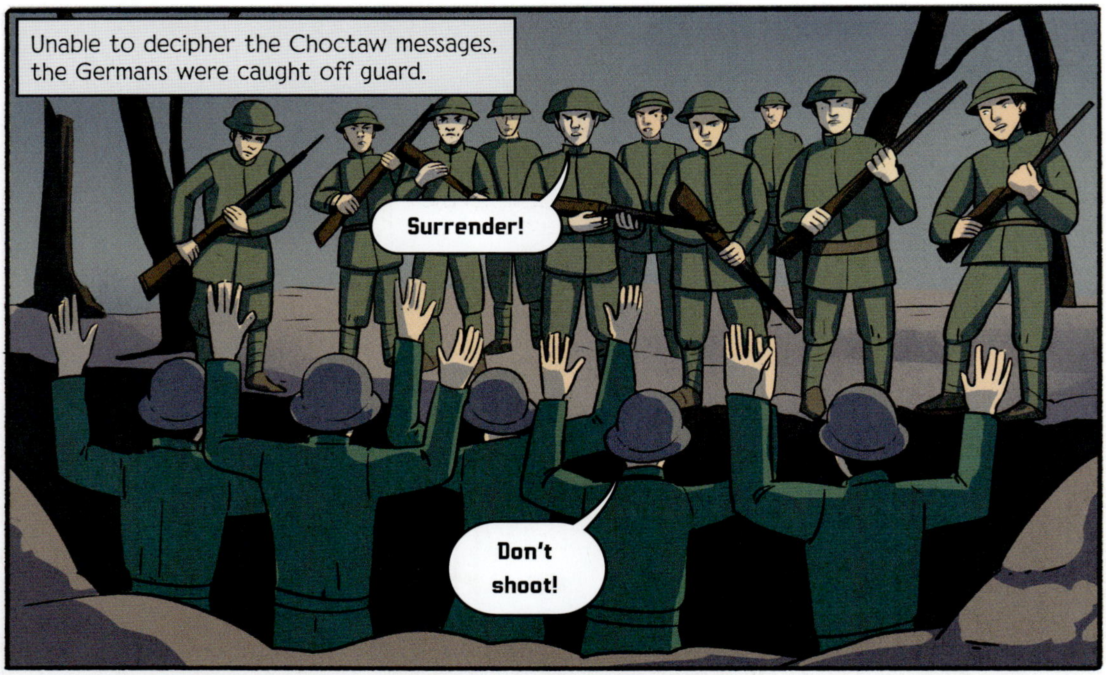
Unable to decipher the Choctaw messages, the Germans were caught off guard.
Surrender!
Don't shoot!

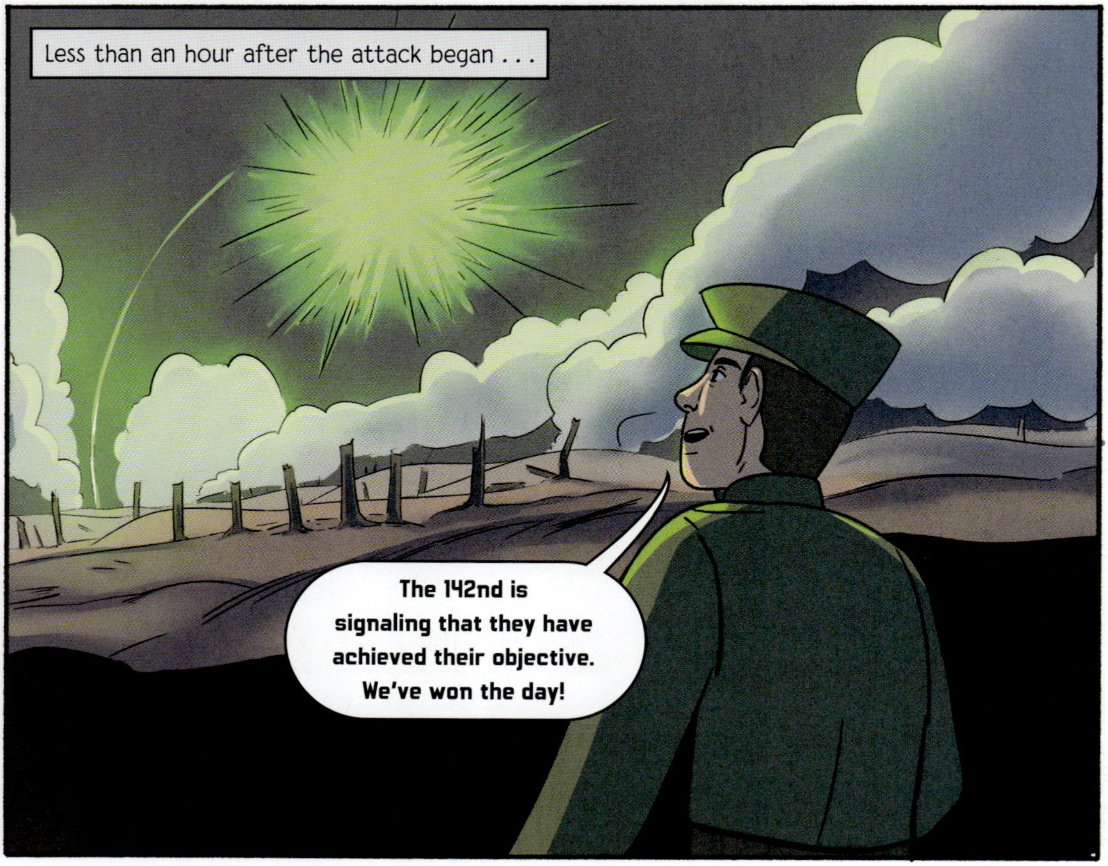
Less than an hour after the attack began . . .
The 142nd is signaling that they have achieved their objective. We've won the day!

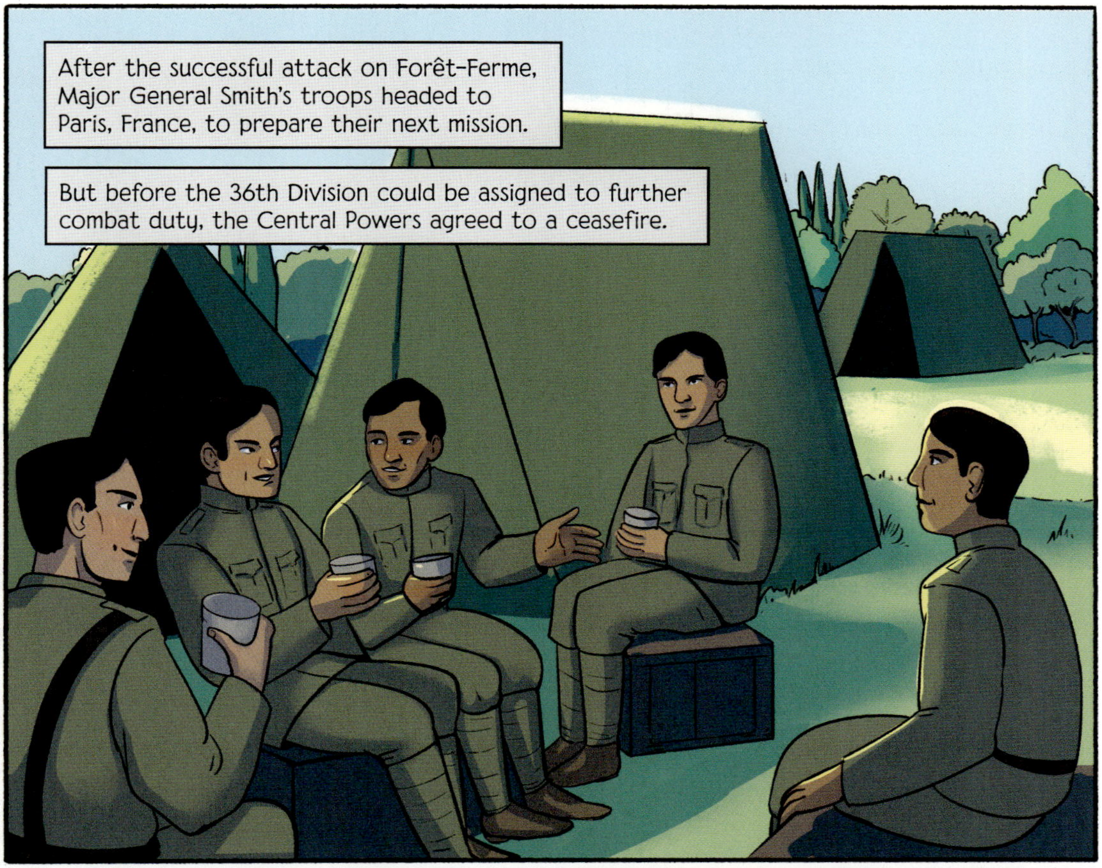
After the successful attack on Forêt-Ferme, Major General Smith's troops headed to Paris, France, to prepare their next mission.
But before the 36th Division could be assigned to further combat duty, the Central Powers agreed to a ceasefire.

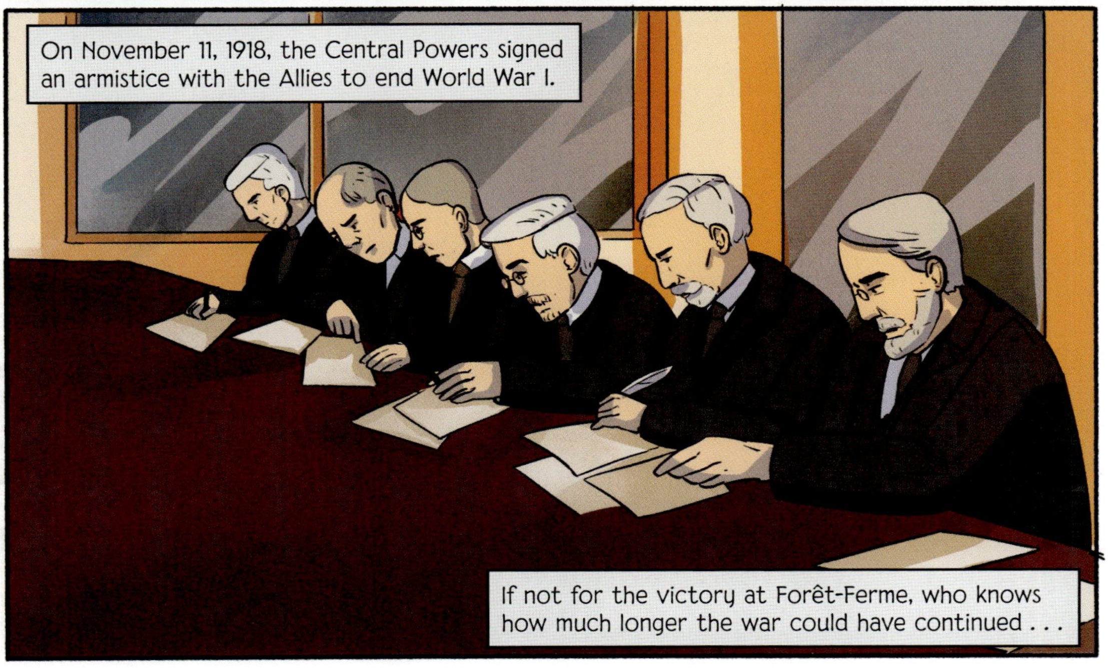
On November 11, 1918, the Central Powers signed an armistice with the Allies to end World War I.
If not for the victory at Forêt-Ferme, who knows how much longer the war could have continued . . .

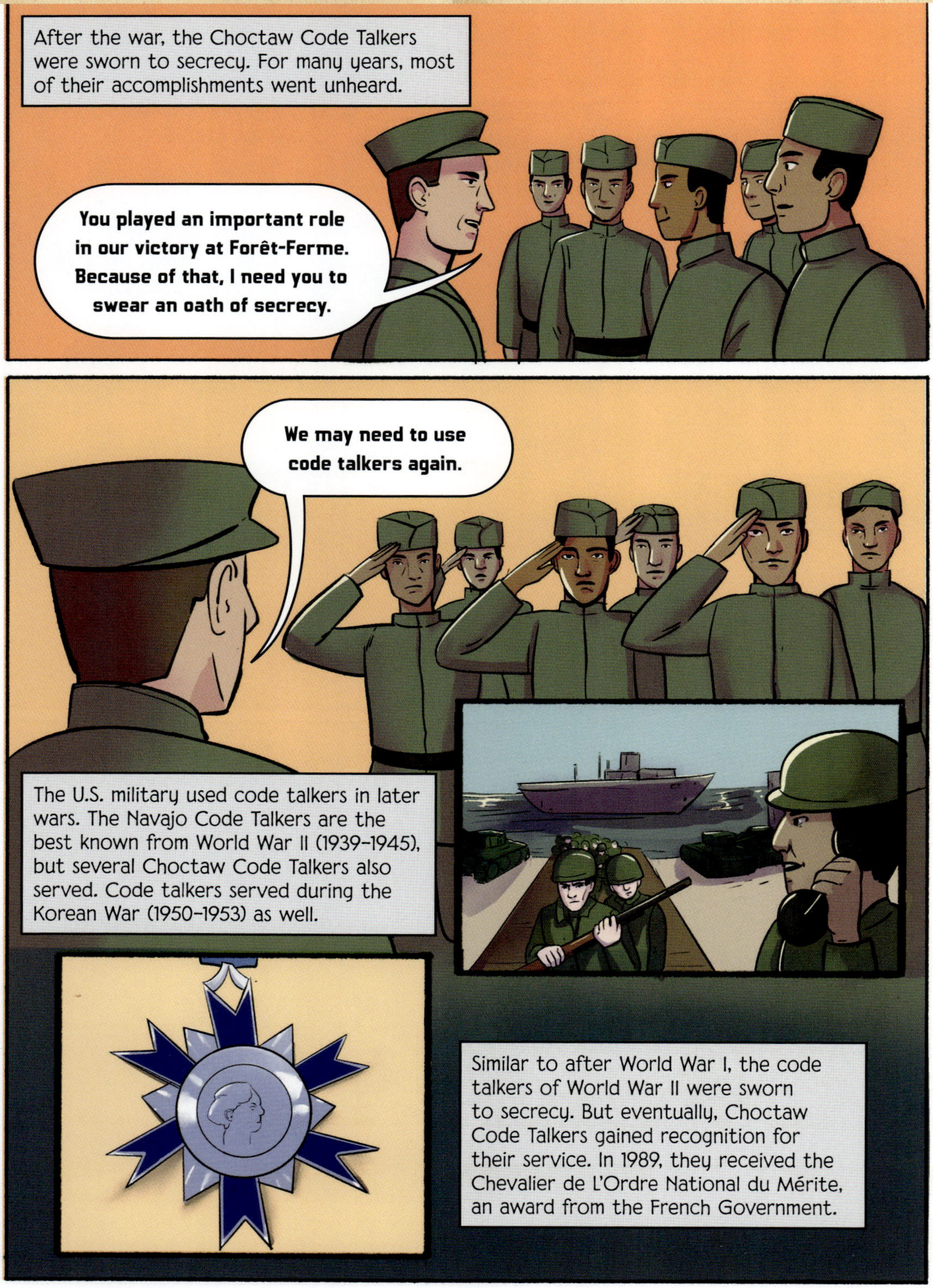

CHAPTER FIVE: AFTER THE WAR

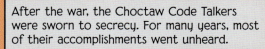

After the war, the Choctaw Code Talkers were sworn to secrecy. For many years, most of their accomplishments went unheard.

"You played an important role in our victory at Forêt-Ferme. Because of that, I need you to swear an oath of secrecy."

"We may need to use code talkers again."

The U.S. military used code talkers in later wars. The Navajo Code Talkers are the best known from World War II (1939–1945), but several Choctaw Code Talkers also served. Code talkers served during the Korean War (1950–1953) as well.

Similar to after World War I, the code talkers of World War II were sworn to secrecy. But eventually, Choctaw Code Talkers gained recognition for their service. In 1989, they received the Chevalier de L'Ordre National du Mérite, an award from the French Government.

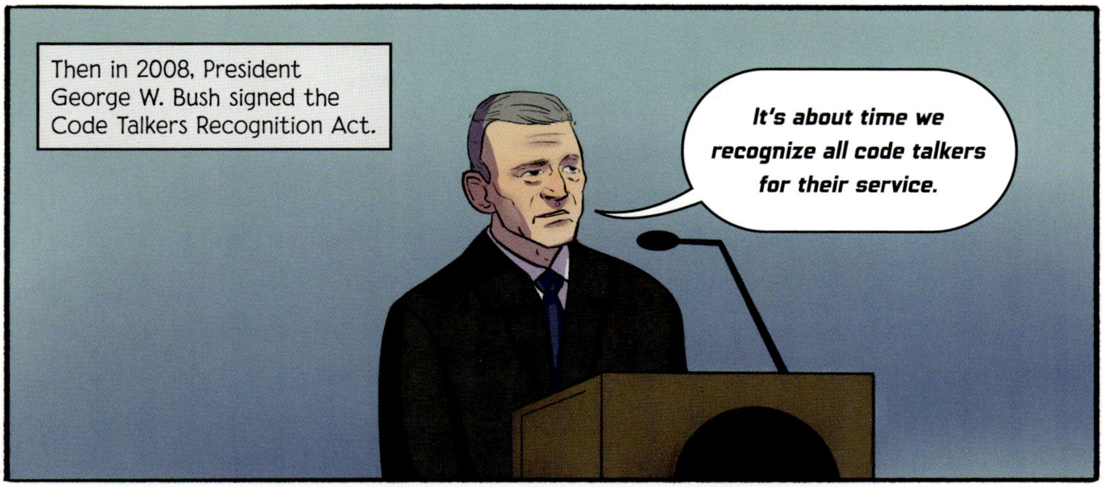
Then in 2008, President George W. Bush signed the Code Talkers Recognition Act.
It's about time we recognize all code talkers for their service.

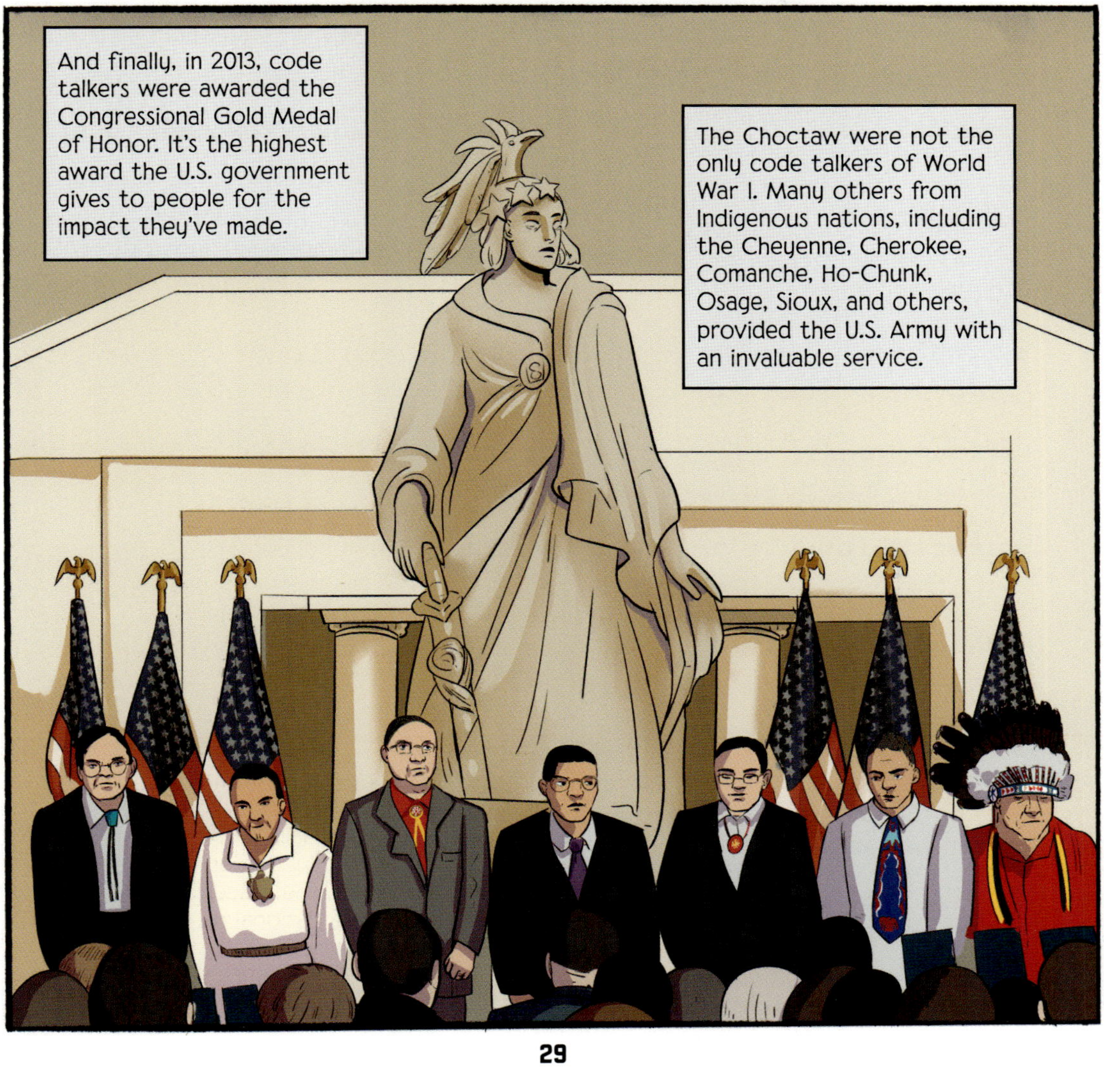
And finally, in 2013, code talkers were awarded the Congressional Gold Medal of Honor. It's the highest award the U.S. government gives to people for the impact they've made.
The Choctaw were not the only code talkers of World War I. Many others from Indigenous nations, including the Cheyenne, Cherokee, Comanche, Ho-Chunk, Osage, Sioux, and others, provided the U.S. Army with an invaluable service.

GLOSSARY

armistice (AR-muh-stis)—an agreement made by both sides to stop fighting in a war

artillery (ar-TIL-uh-ree)—large guns or cannons used in war

ceasefire (SEES-fahy-ur)—a temporary stop to fighting in a war, agreed upon by both sides

decipher (dih-SYE-fur)—to change into an understandable form, or decode

division (di-VIZH-un)—a large group of soldiers who fight together in the army

Indigenous (in-DIHJ-uh-nuhss)—the earliest known people of a place and especially of a place that was colonized

migrate (MYE-grayt)—to move from one country, place, or area to another

offensive (uh-FEN-siv)—a planned attack in a war, usually to push the enemy back

reservation (reh-zur-VAY-shuhn)—land reserved for use by an Indigenous tribe

treaty (TREE-tee)—a formal agreement between countries, usually to end a war

trench (TRENCH)—a long, narrow ditch soldiers dig to protect themselves from enemy fire during war

READ MORE

Braun, Eric. *Can You Survive a World War I Escape?* North Mankato, MN: Capstone, 2023.

Hoena, Blake. *Navajo Code Talkers: Top Secret Messengers of World War II.* North Mankato, MN: Capstone, 2020.

Medina, Nico. *What Was World War I?* New York: Penguin Workshop, 2023.

INTERNET SITES

Choctaw Nation of Oklahoma: Code Talkers
choctawnation.com/about/history/code-talkers

National Museum of the United States Army: World War I Code Talkers
thenmusa.org/articles/world-war-i-code-talkers

Oklahoma Historical Society: The Encyclopedia of Oklahoma History and Culture: Code Talkers
okhistory.org/publications/enc/entry?entry=CO013

OTHER TITLES IN THE SERIES:

ELITE MILITARY UNITS
BUSHMASTERS
ELITE COMBAT TEAM of World War II

ELITE MILITARY UNITS
HARLEM HELLFIGHTERS
ELITE INFANTRY SOLDIERS of World War I

ELITE MILITARY UNITS
NISEI SOLDIERS
ELITE FIGHTING FORCE of World War II

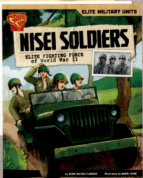

ABOUT THE AUTHOR

Blake A. Hoena grew up in central Wisconsin, where he wrote stories about robots conquering the moon and trolls lumbering around the woods behind his parents' house. He now lives in Minnesota and enjoys writing about fun things like history, space aliens, and superheroes. Blake has written more than 50 chapter books and dozens of graphic novels for children.

ABOUT THE ILLUSTRATOR

Maddi Coyne is an illustrator based in New England. She grew up reading comics and manga, and now loves making comics for young readers. She graduated from Massachusetts College of Art and Design. When not drawing, she's probably reading, learning new things, or playing D&D with her friends.